An Uncompromising Life

An Uncompromising Life

by
John MacArthur, Jr.

MOODY PRESS
CHICAGO

Library of Congress Cataloging in Publication Data

MacArthur, John, 1939-
    An uncompromising life / by John MacArthur, Jr.
      p.   cm. — (John MacArthur's Bible studies)
    Includes indexes.
    ISBN 0-8024-5364-3
    1. Bible.   O.T.   Daniel—Criticism, interpretation, etc.
I. Title.   II. Series: MacArthur, John, 1939-   Bible studies.
BS1555.2.M33   1988
224'.506—dc19   88-19904
                                                        CIP

2 3 4 5 6 7 8 Printing/EP/Year 95 94 93 92 91 90

Printed in the United States of America

Contents

These Bible studies are taken from messages delivered by Pastor-Teacher John MacArthur, Jr., at Grace Community Church in Panorama City, California. The recorded messages themselves may be purchased as a series or individually. Please request the current price list by writing to:

WORD OF GRACE COMMUNICATIONS
P.O. Box 4000
Panorama City, CA 91412

Or call the following toll-free number:
1-800-55-GRACE

1

An Uncompromising Life

Outline

Introduction
A. The Compromise of Society
    1. Its expression within society
    2. Its emulation among the saved
B. The Call of Scripture
    1. The call established
    2. The Corinthians exhorted
    3. The consequences explained
       a) Compromise destroys our worship
          (1) Hebrews 13:12-15
          (2) 1 John 2:15
          (3) James 4:4
       b) Compromise destroys our service
    4. The commitment exemplified

Lesson
I. The Plight (vv. 1-2)
A. The Sorrow of the Situation
    1. Jerusalem besieged
    2. Judah warned
B. The Setting of the Scene
    1. Daniel's deportation to Babylon
    2. Nebuchadnezzar's defeat of Jerusalem
II. The Plot (vv. 3-7)
A. Taking the Hostages (v. 3)
    1. The command to Ashpenaz
    2. The children of Israel

Introduction

The first nine verses of Daniel 1 describe the background of an uncompromising life: "In the third year of the reign of Jehoiakim, king of Judah, came Nebuchadnezzar, king of Babylon, unto Jerusalem, and besieged it. And the Lord gave Jehoiakim, king of Judah, into his hand, with part of the vessels of the house of God, which he carried into the land of Shinar to the house of his god; and he brought the vessels into the treasure house of his god. And the king spoke unto Ashpenaz, the master of his eunuchs, that he should bring certain of the children of Israel, and of the king's seed, and of the princes, youths in whom was no blemish, but well favored, and skillful in all wisdom, and gifted in knowledge, and understanding science, and such as had ability in them to stand in the king's palace, and whom they might teach the learning and the tongue of the Chaldeans. And the king appointed them a daily provision of the king's food, and of the wine which he drank, so nourishing them three years that, at the end of them, they might stand before the king. Now among these were of the children of Judah, Daniel, Hananiah, Mishael, and Azariah, unto whom the prince of the eunuchs gave names; for he gave unto Daniel the name of Belteshazzar; and to Hananiah, of Shadrach; and to Mishael, of Meshach; and to Azariah, of Abed-nego. But Daniel purposed in his heart that he would not defile himself with the portion of the king's food, nor with the wine which he drank; therefore, he requested of the prince of the eunuchs that he might not defile himself. Now God had brought Daniel into favor and compassion with the prince of the eunuchs."

A. The Compromise of Society

   1. Its expression within society

   We live in an era of compromise. In fact, I believe that from the time our lives begin, we start to learn the art of compromise. We follow the path of least resistance much of the time. We often hold a conviction until it stands in the way of our comfort or have a standard as long as it doesn't violate something we wish to do. If we can get by with a little less than our best, we'll often do it. If we can cheat on the principles we claim to follow, we'll sometimes do that, too, if it helps accomplish our goals. Such a self-centered, worldly perspective is so widespread that we essentially live in a world of compromise.

   Our motto could be, "If it works for you, do it." Today our society has abandoned moral standards and Christian principles. We no longer are concerned about biblical morality. The majority of our society couldn't care less about what God has to say. We are left only with the philosophy of expedience, or pragmatism: Whatever works or accomplishes your goal is what you should do.

And thus we easily give up our consciences and convictions to gain some practical end. Our society seems to have little conscience left, with little sense of guilt or remorse.

We often see politicians who appeared to have such high standards prior to their election compromise those standards when they find themselves in office. We find the same thing often true in business, from corporate executives down to salespeople. Lawyers, who should be the conscience of any society, often compromise if it gains a certain end. Leaders in all walks of life will often do the same. As individuals we learn to lie, cheat, steal, and shade the truth, doing whatever is necessary to receive what we want. Compromise becomes a way of life.

2. Its emulation among the saved

When we in the church encounter a confrontation, sometimes our principles are compromised because we don't want to offend someone, be obtrusive, or speak what we believe. Perhaps the spirit of compromise is nowhere more obvious than when you're in a conversation where you know you should proclaim Christ, yet you remain silent.

Indeed, this philosophy and practice of compromise has found its way into the church. Some have compromised with the world so repeatedly that they don't understand what the compromises are anymore. Whenever the world comes up with something new, the church invariably follows it. If the world has a hippie movement, we have a hippie movement. If the world has a rock-music movement, we have one. If the world has a woman's liberation movement, we have one too. We have so long compromised with the world and become so engulfed in its materialistic viewpoint that little possibility exists that we can understand what an uncompromising life means. We fight to be separated from the world, yet we are unable to define what that separation means because we've been brainwashed by the system. We have accepted the world's value systems and have indulged ourselves in them. Even when we know the Bible prohibits a certain activity, we often do it anyway.

Recently a couple who desired to be married came in for counseling. But after finding no biblical justification for their marriage, we counseled them that they had no basis to be married. However, they simply went somewhere else to be married. Compromise is the inability to deal with the biblical data because we are overwhelmed with our own personal desires. Therefore we substitute ourselves in the place of God. We learn the art of compromise when we indulge ourselves in the world's priorities.

B. The Call of Scripture

Scripture calls us to the opposite of compromise. From one end of the Bible to the other, God clearly commands His people to live apart from the world.

1. The call established

When God established the nation Israel, He built into the Israelites' daily living the principle of separation from the world. Their religious observances throughout the year served as safeguards to prevent them, as a unique people (Deut. 14:2), from intermingling with pagans. God has called all His people to be separate from the world (2 Pet. 2:9).

We have a standard that isn't compatible with the world, yet we easily compromise that standard. We abandon our absolutes and allow our perspective to become worldly. However, we need to remind ourselves that God is an uncompromising God. He never compromises His absolute truths and principles for the purpose of expediency. God always lives according to His Word. Psalm 138:2 says, "Thou hast magnified thy word above all thy name." God has made His nature submissive to His Word. And His Word is the basis of integrity in a believer. As the Holy One, God has exalted His Word above His name and has committed Himself to that very Word. As His children, we are to do the same.

2. The Corinthians exhorted

Second Corinthians 6:17-18 provides a summary in the New Testament relative to this kind of separation from the world: "Wherefore, come out from among them [the idolatrous and unrighteous people], and be ye separate, saith the Lord, and touch not the unclean thing; and I will receive you, and will be a Father unto you, and ye shall be my sons and daughters, saith the Lord Almighty." God is holy and uncompromising, and He instructs His people that if they are to truly manifest that they are His, they must also be separated (holy) and uncompromising in their lives.

3. The consequences explained

When Christians compromise with the world, it has devastating results in two areas.

a) Compromise destroys our worship

(1) Hebrews 13:12-15—"Wherefore, Jesus also, that he might sanctify ["set apart" or "separate"] the people with his own blood, suffered outside the gate." In the sacrificial system of Israel, when it was time to slay the lamb for the sins of the people, those sins were symbolically placed upon another animal that was then taken outside the city. Hence, they were separated from the people. Likewise, Jesus died outside the walls—separated from the city. If Christ separated Himself to purchase a separated people, "let us go forth, therefore, unto him outside the camp, bearing his reproach" (v. 13). We must follow the example of Christ and live a separated life. "For we have no continuing city, but we seek one to come. By him, therefore, let us offer the sacrifice of praise to God continually" (vv. 14-15). You can't worship unless you're living a separated life. Don't come to God with your praise, thanksgiving, and good deeds unless you abandon worldliness.

(2) 1 John 2:15—"Love not the world, neither the things that are in the world. If any man love the world, the love of the Father is not in him."

(3) James 4:4—"Know ye not that the friendship of the world is enmity with God? Whosoever therefore, will be a friend of the world is the enemy of God."

We are called, then, to a separated life—separated from the defilements of the world. When we are not separated, compromise destroys our worship.

b) Compromise destroys our service

We can't serve the Lord if we compromise; it makes us useless. Second Timothy 2:20 says, "But in a great house there are not only vessels of gold and of silver, but also of wood and of earth; and some to honor, and some to dishonor." In your home you may have old, chipped utensils as well as fine china and silver. Likewise in God's church, utensils (Gk., *skeuos*) —vessels of honor—will be used. Now if you want to be a utensil that God takes pleasure in using, then you must "purge [yourself] from these [false teachers and false standards of living]" (v. 21). You must separate yourself "from iniquity" (v. 19) and "flee . . . youthful lusts" (v. 22) and "foolish and unlearned questions . . . , knowing that they breed strifes" (v. 23). Only then can you "be a vessel unto honor, sanctified, and fit for the Master's use" (v. 21).

God calls us to be separate. Unless we are living a separated life, we are destroying our worship and our service to Him. A purging and a purification in our lives must take place. Sometimes this will mean taking drastic steps.

A yacht on the Niagara River broke away from the dock and began to drift. The people on board became panicstricken as the boat rapidly headed toward Niagara Falls. They could hear the thundering sound of the falls

13

immediately ahead of them. Then the skipper blew a hole in the hull of the boat with dynamite. Immediately the boat began to sink and lodged itself on the bottom of the river. The people were rescued as they clung to the boat.

That's what must happen in our lives. Somewhere along the line, we as believers must sink the ship of compromise and worldliness, or we'll find ourselves rapidly moving toward disaster.

4. The commitment exemplified

God calls us to a standard of holiness. This standard of commitment is exemplified in the lives of many individuals in the Bible.

a) By Jesus

Hebrews 7:26 says of Christ, "For such an high priest was fitting for us, who is holy, harmless, undefiled, separate from sinners." Jesus is the pattern for a lifetime of commitment to holiness.

b) By Moses

Moses also made that commitment to a separated life. Hebrews 11:25-27 says, "Choosing rather to suffer affliction with the people of God than to enjoy the pleasures of sin for a season, esteeming the reproach of Christ greater riches than the treasures in Egypt; for he had respect unto the recompense of the reward. By faith he forsook Egypt, not fearing the wrath of the king; for he endured, as seeing him who is invisible." Moses chose God and heaven over Pharaoh and the earth. He chose affliction in God's will over the riches of Egypt outside of God's will.

c) By Ruth

Ruth made a similar commitment: "They lifted up their voice, and wept again; and Orpah kissed her mother-in-law, but Ruth clung to her. And she said, Behold, thy sister-in-law is gone back unto her people, and unto her gods; return thou after thy sister-in-law [Naomi encouraged Ruth to follow Orpah back to her former life among the Moabites]. And Ruth said, Entreat me not to leave thee, or to turn away from following after thee; for where thou goest, I will go; and where thou lodgest, I will lodge: thy people shall be my people, and thy God, my God. Where thou diest, will I die, and there will I be buried; the Lord do so to me, and more also, if anything but death part thee and me. When she saw that she was steadfastly determined to go with her, then she ceased speaking unto her" (Ruth 1:14-18). Ruth was saying, "I will not return to my former life. I am committed to you and the God you represent."

d) By David

David made a similar commitment: "I have sworn and I will perform it, that I will keep thy righteous ordinances. . . . Depart from me, ye evildoers; for I will keep the commandments of my God" (Ps. 119:106, 115).

e) By Barnabas

Acts 11:23 says of Barnabas, a man of God instrumental in the early church, "Who, when he came, and had seen the grace of God, was glad, and exhorted them all, that with purpose of heart they would cling unto the Lord." Barnabas told the early church to be uncompromising and to cleave to the Lord.

f) By Daniel

There is no better example of the character of an uncompromising spirit than Daniel. In fact, Ezekiel, who was a contemporary of Daniel, must have been aware of this because when God listed the great men of righteousness in history, He said they were "Noah, Daniel, and Job" (Ezek. 14:14). He included Daniel although the other two had died and Daniel was still alive. Rarely does a living man receive that kind of honor. Daniel must have been an exceptional person.

Lesson

I. THE PLIGHT (vv. 1-2)

"In the third year of the reign of Jehoiakim, king of Judah, came Nebuchadnezzar, king of Babylon, unto Jerusalem, and besieged it. And the Lord gave Jehoiakim, king of Judah, into his hand, with part of the vessels of the house of God, which he carried into the land of Shinar to the house of his god; and he brought the vessels into the treasure house of his god."

A. The Sorrow of the Situation

1. Jerusalem besieged

The book of Daniel begins on a sorrowful note by recording for us the first of three Babylonian captivities. The Northern Kingdom of Israel had long gone into captivity. Now judgment came to Judah, the remaining Southern Kingdom of Israel, because of its unfaithfulness and disobedience to God. Nebuchadnezzar, who essentially ruled that part of the world as king of Babylon, besieged Jerusalem and took some of its inhabitants captive in a series of three separate deportations (the first one occurring during the time of Jehoiakim in 605 B.C.).

2. Judah warned

But God didn't bring judgment without warning the people. First he warned them through the prophets, who constantly reminded them that if they didn't repent, inevitable judgment would come. He also warned them by allowing the Assyrians to invade Israel, giving them a taste of foreign oppression. God finally warned them by taking the Northern Kingdom into captivity. They should have learned when they saw what happened to the North, but they didn't. They continued in their sin. God was patient, merciful, and gracious with them, yet the same God who says in Genesis 6:3, "My Spirit shall not always strive with man," stopped striving with Judah and brought judgment on them by taking them into captivity.

B. The Setting of the Scene

1. Daniel's deportation to Babylon

Daniel, his friends, and other young men were taken in the first deportation to Babylon. Evidently, the whole nation wasn't taken into captivity at that time because God wanted Daniel in a position of authority before the rest of the captives of the later deportations arrived.

2. Nebuchadnezzar's defeat of Jerusalem

When Nebuchadnezzar besieged Jerusalem and defeated Jehoiakim, king of Judah, he chose not to dethrone him. Having seen that Jehoiakim had been a willing vassal to Pharaoh of Egypt in the past, Nebuchadnezzar determined he was weak enough to allow him to rule as king without causing any problems.

To prove his power, Nebuchadnezzar stole everything of value out of the house of God. If one could steal treasures from the gods of a foreign power, it was supposedly proof of your greatness. It was reasoned that if a god couldn't defend the utensils of his own temple, then he was powerless. Rulers that conquered nations would invariably gather all the riches from the temples and take them back to their own country to affirm their power over foreign gods (cf. 1 Sam. 5:1-2).

Nebuchadnezzar took the articles from the Jerusalem Temple and placed them in the house of his god, Bel (also known as Baal, Merodach, and Marduk). I believe the reason that this incident was recorded was to show how comprehensive the coming doom was going to be. God wasn't defending Judah anymore; He allowed His own Temple to be robbed.

This must have been a difficult time for Daniel, who, seventy years after his deportation, still faithfully prayed (cf. 6:10) and longed for the city of Jerusalem. You can imagine what must have gone on in his heart at the time he was taken captive.

THE PLOT (vv. 3-7)

The historical background of this passage sets the stage for everything that was going to take place in Daniel's life in Babylon. As Nebuchadnezzar was besieging Jerusalem, he received word that his father had died. So he returned to Babylon, leaving Jehoiakim, king of Judah, in power. But to insure Jehoiakim's loyalty, Nebuchadnezzar took hostages. The first deportation, then, was really not a mass deportation of the people of Judah. He simply took hostages until he could return at a later date and complete his conquest. (Two further deportations occurred in 597 and 586 B.C.)

A. Taking the Hostages (v. 3)

"The king spoke unto Ashpenaz, the master of his eunuchs, that he should bring certain of the children of Israel, and of the king's seed, and of the princes."

1. The command to Ashpenaz

Nebuchadnezzar wanted hostages right out of the princely nobility of the land of Judah, so he commanded Ashpenaz to find them. Some believe Ashpenaz is a proper name, whereas others believe it is merely a title of someone who is a master or overseer. Assuming that it is a proper name, this individual is identified as "the master of his [Nebuchadnezzar's] eunuchs."

Every king had eunuchs—those who served him in his court. Isaiah identified a eunuch as "a dry tree" (56:3). That's because some eunuchs were men who had gone through surgical emasculations and were placed in charge of harems. However, because eunuchs served the king, the term *eunuch* was used for many men who served the king but had not been made eunuchs surgically. For example, although Potiphar is referred to as a eunuch in the Hebrew text, we know he was married because Joseph encountered his wife (Gen. 39:1-12). Daniel may have been a eunuch physically. The king would likely make these young men eunuchs when they entered into his service. This could explain why Daniel, who apparently never married or was identified with a family, served the king for the rest of his life.

Ashpenaz, as "master" (lit., "prince") of the eunuchs, held an important office and was given the task of collecting a group of hostages.

2. The children of Israel

Some historians indicate that somewhere between fifty and seventy-five hostages were taken into captivity. Although they were "of the children of Israel," they were not necessarily from the Northern Kingdom. Because of the migration of the remnant of the northern tribes into the South following the Assyrian invasions in the North, Judah actually embodied the seed from both kingdoms. The hostages were Israelites living in Judah and specifically "of the king's seed, and of the princes." They came from the royal family and the nobility. Nebuchadnezzar used those hostages to control Jehoiakim.

B. Training the Hostages (vv. 4-7)

Nebuchadnezzar wanted to train these young men in his courts to assist him in administering Jewish affairs. He planned to make Judah a vassal state to Babylon. To handle these Jewish people, he wanted to transform some Jewish boys into Chaldeans who would, in turn, be able to administer his rule among the Jews.

1. The selection process (v. 4a)

   a) Physical qualities

      (1) Age

      "Youths."

      This word translated "youths" in Hebrew is *yeladim*. Most commentators agree that the youths were no older than seventeen years old and probably no younger than thirteen or fourteen. At this time Daniel was a teenager. Knowing that Daniel was still serving as a leader in Babylon seventy years later, he must have been quite young—possibly fourteen or fifteen years old. Nebuchadnezzar wanted Jewish youths that he could educate as Chaldeans.

(2) Appearance

"In whom was no blemish, but well favored."

The Hebrew word translated "blemish" (*muum*) refers to a physical blemish. Nebuchadnezzar didn't want anyone who had any physical handicaps; he wanted a flawless physical specimen. The words *well favored* refer particularly to the face, with emphasis on appearance. The youths were evaluated partly on their physical characteristics. This is rather typical. It's probably no coincidence that Saul, the first king of Israel, was the tallest and handsomest man in the country.

b) Mental qualities

(1) "Skillful in all wisdom"

The youths were superior intellectually with an ability to make distinctions and decisions and apply truth in practical situations.

(2) "Gifted in knowledge"

They had superior education. The literal Hebrew translation is "knowers of knowledge." They were good students.

(3) "Understanding science"

The phrase "understanding science" in Hebrew carries the idea of an ability to correlate facts—bringing information together and making wise decisions. That is essentially what science does: it draws conclusions from the correlation of data.

c) Social qualities

"Such as had the ability in them to stand in the king's palace."

Not only was Nebuchadnezzar concerned with the physical and the mental characteristics of the young men, but also with their social qualities. They required the poise, manners, and social graces necessary to stand in the king's palace.

When the world looks for people to fill its criteria, it evaluates their physical, mental, and social qualities. The Babylonians had little concern about character or spirituality; they weren't interested in virtue or morality. They wanted the smartest, best looking, and most courteous young men they could find.

2. The educational process (v. 4b)

"Whom they might teach the learning and the tongue of the Chaldeans."

The term *Chaldeans* is used interchangeably with the term *Babylonians*. Originally the Chaldeans were a separate group, but as the Babylonian Empire grew, Chaldean astrology, sciences, and other learning disciplines dominated the empire to such an extent that the two terms became synonymous. Therefore the plan was to make them full-fledged Babylonians or Chaldeans through the education of the Chaldeans.

a) Languages

The Chaldean language was a powerful and important language in that day. Because the Jews did not converse in that tongue, they would have to learn it to effectively communicate in that part of the world. *The International Standard Bible Encyclopedia* says that "the learning of the Chaldeans . . . comprised the old languages of Babylonia (the two dialects of Sumerian, with a certain knowledge of Kassite, which seems to have been allied to the Hittite; and other languages of the immediate neighborhood)" ([Chicago: Howard-Severance, 1925], p. 591).

b) Sciences

The International Standard Bible Encyclopedia says that their learning also included "knowledge of astronomy and astrology; mathematics, which their sexagesimal system of numeration seems to have facilitated; and a certain amount of natural history" (p. 591).

c) Humanities

"To this must be added a store of mythological learning, including legends of the Creation [and] the Flood [Chaldean religious legends acknowledged a plurality of gods]. . . . They had likewise a good knowledge of agriculture, and were no mean architects, as the many celebrated buildings of Babylon show" (p. 591). The most outstanding example was the Hanging Gardens of Babylon, one of the seven wonders of the ancient world.

These young men were to be exposed to all of this learning—architectural, agricultural, linguistic, theological, and historical. They were to become erudite Chaldeans through brainwashing.

Are Young People Being Brainwashed?

What the Babylonians attempted to do is not unlike what many professors and college textbooks attempt to do to young people today. They sometimes try to take away their faith, rob them of their heritage, and reform them with godless, humanistic information. Even some seminaries in our country that once held up the Word of God have abandoned its authority. They are guilty of brainwashing their students to believe that human wisdom is superior to God's Word.

Moses may have gone through a similar process in Egypt when he "learned in all the wisdom of the Egyptians" (Acts 7:22). But some people cannot be corrupted, and Moses and Daniel were two of them. The universities and the seminaries of the Chaldeans were attempting to destroy everything that Daniel and his friends knew of God and of their divinely strategic heritage as His chosen people.

A similar effort is being made in modern education. From the time young people go to school, many teachers present them with a humanistic and atheistic system of values. These values are designed by Satan to undermine the truth of God's Word.

3. The nourishment process (vv. 5-7)

　　a) Obligation for the future (vv. 5-6)

　　　　(1) The king's food

"The king appointed them a daily provision of the king's food [delicacies]."

The *Revised Standard Version* correctly translates "the king's food" as "rich food." Why were they to be fed the king's rich food? One of the most basic elements of brainwashing is creating a sense of obligation. The Babylonians did so by making the young Jews' sustenance dependent on their captors. Once the Babylonians established a sense of well-being in their captives, those captives would be conditioned to do anything necessary to retain such abundant provisions. The Babylonians wanted to seduce the hostages into being obligated to serve them. Therefore they raised their standard of living to the point where they would never want to return to their old lifestyles.

　　　　(2) The king's wine

"And of the wine which he drank, so nourishing them three years that, at the end of them, they might stand before the king."

After three years of the king's food, it was hoped that they would be motivated to serve the king. The phrase "stand before the king" means to serve him. That shows us service was the goal of Nebuchadnezzar's conditioning process. This idea of service is clearly implied in the phrase "stand before." For example, when angels stand before

the throne of God, they are waiting for a commis-
sion to serve (Luke 1:19). Jeremiah the prophet
stood before God when he was commissioned to
speak to Judah (Jer. 15:19). Nebuchadnezzar believed the young men would serve him out of obligation to uphold a luxurious standard of living.

If you've ever eaten unusually expensive food,
perhaps you've gotten a taste of how tempting
such a diet can be. Out of the fifty to seventy-five
young men who were taken as hostages, apparently only four didn't yield to this dietary brainwashing process. "Now among these were of the
children of Judah, Daniel, Hananiah, Mishael,
and Azariah" (v. 6). The phrase "among these"
indicates that many more were there, but only
four stood up for what they believed in. Not
many people in the world will resist the world's
effort to brainwash them.

b) Obliteration of the past (v. 7)

"Unto whom the prince of the eunuchs gave names;
for he gave unto Daniel the name of Belteshazzar;
and to Hananiah, of Shadrach; and to Mishael, of
Meshach; and to Azariah, of Abed-nego."

The Hebrew names of the hostages were changed to
Chaldean names so that they would forget their
roots. Once a person's past is forgotten, so is his
identity.

Cutting people off from their heritage is not a new
ploy. Joseph's name was changed to Zaphenath-pan-
eah in Egypt (Gen. 41:45). Esther's name was
changed to Hadassah when she was taken captive
into another society (Esther 2:7). Daniel's name,
which means "God is judge," was changed to Belteshazzar ("Bel provides" or "Bel's prince"). The association to Yahweh (God) was changed to Bel or Baal
in an effort to erase his belief in God. Hananiah's
name ("the Lord is gracious") was changed to Shad-

rach, apparently to exalt Aku, another chief Babylonian deity. Mishael's name ("Who is what the Lord is?") was altered to Meshach ("Who is what Aku is?"). And finally, Azariah's name ("the Lord is my helper") was changed to Abednego, "the servant of Nebo" (Nebo being the son of Baal).

In each case, those four Hebrew names reflected a godly upbringing. For this reason, they may have stood out among the rest of the captives. Since only a remnant of believing people remained in Judah, these four may have been among the few who had a godly heritage.

The Babylonians were trying to substitute their demonic pantheon in God's place.

III. THE PURPOSE (v. 8a)

"But Daniel purposed in his heart that he would not defile himself with the portion of the king's food, nor with the wine which he drank."

In spite of the fact that Daniel was only around fourteen years old, he "purposed in his heart" (lit., "laid upon his heart") to abstain from the dietary conditioning of the Babylonians.

A. The Acceptance

These young men were to be influenced by three distinctly heathen practices: they were to be taught human wisdom, they were to be given heathen names, and they were to be fed heathen food. They accepted only the first two.

1. Heathen education

Babylonian education cannot be considered entirely evil. They learned many helpful principles of architecture and science. They allowed themselves a secular education. However, we must be careful to sort the good from the bad and the true from the false by following a divine standard.

2. Heathen names

Although their names were changed, that wouldn't change the fact that their original names were written in God's Book as His children.

B. The Abstinence

The third aspect of conditioning is where they drew the line. Daniel said he would not defile (pollute or stain) himself with the king's food and wine. Whereas there were no strict prohibitions in the Word of God against taking a heathen name or learning what other people had to teach, strict prohibitions about what a Jew could eat and drink did exist. Daniel refused to disobey the Word of God. What is the character of an uncompromising life? It is a commitment to the Word of God. Daniel abstained from eating the king's food for two major reasons.

1. Jewish dietary laws

Jewish food had to be prepared in a certain way with the blood properly drained off. And the Jews differentiated between clean and unclean animals (Lev. 11). The Babylonians had no such distinction. They feasted on pork as a delicacy and ate other meats that were forbidden to a Jew. Even the preparation of their food was not fitting for a Jew. Part of God's purpose for dietary laws was to keep His people from being corrupted by pagan practice. God's intention was to restrict the possibility of Israelites intermingling with pagans.

2. Pagan idolatrous customs

The Old Testament command was reiterated many times that Israel was not to tolerate idolatry of any kind or associate with people who worshiped idols (e.g., Deut. 7). The food and wine served at the king's table would have been offered to the Babylonian gods. If Daniel and his friends were to eat that food, they would be participating in a pagan feast. But they took their stand on Scripture and obeyed the biblical mandate. Such is the character of an uncompromising life. Daniel chose not to defile or pollute himself by disobeying Scripture.

Conclusion

A. The Reasons for Compromise

Daniel had every reason to compromise. First, he was only a youth. He was also away from home, where no one could question his actions. He was responsible for himself. Furthermore, having been taught to obey authority, Daniel might have felt obligated to accept the king's dietary provision. If he wanted to advance in the kingdom as a promising young man of character, it would demand unwavering obedience to what the king said. In the event he disobeyed, the king would be angry, and no one would want to fall out of favor with a king who threw rebels into fiery furnaces. Finally, Daniel might have believed God had let Israel down by allowing the young men to be taken captive. Therefore Daniel had every reason to compromise.

B. The Refusal to Compromise

Daniel didn't compromise because he had integrity. He would learn the king's language and the sciences of the Chaldeans. He would even accept a pagan name, but he would never accept the life-style. Yet in his refusal Daniel didn't become angry and bitter. In fact, verse 9 says, "God had brought Daniel into favor and compassion with the prince of the eunuchs." Daniel held his convictions with love. The character of an uncompromising life is based upon an absolute obedience to the principles of God's Word. When the Bible says something, don't compromise; hold to your conviction with love. When you live an uncompromising life, God will use you.

I remember reading a story about a wealthy Englishman who had a collection of rare violins. One instrument was of such quality and value that early twentieth-century Austrian violinist Fritz Kreisler desired to purchase it. But the owner was reluctant. One day Kreisler begged for permission to play the violin. The request was granted and the great violinist played as only one of his talent could. He poured his soul into his music. As the master artist played, the Englishman stood enchanted. When Kreisler finished, not a word was spoken as he loosened the bow and the strings and placed the instrument in its case with the gentleness of a mother putting her baby to bed. Then the owner exclaimed, "Take the violin, Kreisler. It is yours. I have no right to keep it. It ought to belong to one who can make such beautiful music upon it."

God can make beautiful music with your life as He did with Daniel's. But you've got to give Him your life. Be like Daniel and live an uncompromising life based on the principles of God's Word.

Focusing on the Facts

1. Briefly describe the philosophy of compromise in our society (see pp. 9-10).
2. As Christians, why do we often allow some of our greatest principles to be shoved into the background (see pp. 10-11)?
3. Why is it difficult for Christians in our society to understand what an uncompromising life really means (see pp. 10-11)?
4. Compromise is the inability to deal with the biblical data because we are overwhelmed with our own _____ _____ (see p. 11).
5. How does God call His people to live (see p. 11)?
6. How do we know that God lives according to His Word (see p. 11; Ps. 138:2)?
7. How are we to live as children of a holy and uncompromising God (see p. 12; 2 Cor. 6:17-18)?
8. What are the two consequences of compromising Christians (see pp. 12-13)?
9. How can we "be a vessel unto honor, sanctified, and fit for the master's use" (2 Tim. 2:21; see p. 13)?
10. What did Moses do that revealed his uncompromising spirit (see p. 14; Heb. 11:25-27)?
11. What in Ezekiel shows that God considered Daniel to be a great man of righteousness (see p. 15; Ezek. 14:14)?
12. Describe the situation with which the book of Daniel begins (see p. 16).

13. What is the significance of a conqueror taking away the riches out of a temple of a foreign power (see p. 17)?
14. Why did Nebuchadnezzar command that hostages be taken (see p. 18)?
15. On what bases did the Babylonians evaluate the Jewish youths (see pp. 19-21)?
16. How would the conditioning with the king's rich food create a sense of obligation (see pp. 23-24; cf. Prov. 23:1-3)?
17. Out of the many young Jewish men who were taken captive, how many stood up for what they believed (see p. 24)?
18. How did Nebuchadnezzar seek to erase the heritage of the youths (see pp. 24-25)?
19. What could have been Daniel's reason for accepting Babylonian education and names (see pp. 25-26)?
20. From a biblical perspective, why did Daniel abstain from the king's food (see pp. 26-27)?
21. What is the character of an uncompromising life (see p. 27)?
22. What is amazing about Daniel's decision not to compromise (see p. 27)?
23. What characterized Daniel's refusal to accept the Babylonian life-style (see pp. 27-28)?

Pondering the Principles

1. Compromise is such a part of our society that we seldom are aware of it. Think about the family, work, or governmental standards you have contact with. Do you profess to honor the integrity of the family yet actually do things that pull it apart? Have you ever permanently "borrowed" something from work, rationalizing that they "owed" it to you? Do you remember disregarding a law because you were in a hurry or because you thought no one would ever find out? With a little self-evaluation, you can see how commonplace compromise can be in our daily lives. Think back to a time you compromised. What do you believe was the bottom line of your motivation to act as you did? Was it a selfish consideration, where you believed that if you abided by a certain principle, that you would be cheating yourself out of what you believed you deserved? Was it an assumption that God wasn't concerned or wasn't able to meet the real need at hand? Maybe it was an attempt to speed up God's time schedule because you wanted an immediate solution. Read Genesis 15:1-6 and 16:1-6. How did

Sarah and Abraham compromise? What was one consequence of circumventing God's promise (see Gen. 16:12; cf. Ps. 83:1-6)? How did Abraham later show that he didn't need to compromise (see Gen. 22:1-18; cf. Heb. 11:17-19)?

2. We often compromise because the desire to please ourselves takes precedence over our desire to please God. Paul tells Christians that they should "walk as children of light . . . trying to learn what is pleasing to the Lord" (Eph. 5:8b, 10, NASB*). Note that this exhortation gives you the idea that such learning should be a continual process. In what ways are you learning to please the Lord? Where would you go to find out what pleases Him? Take time to memorize verse 10 so that the next time you are tempted to compromise, the Spirit will bring this principle to mind and help you stand firm.

3. Has your worship or service to God been hindered because you've compromised moral and other biblical principles? Review the verses discussed on pages 12-13. Memorize either 1 John 2:15 or James 4:4 because you may often find yourself in the midst of a battle of allegiance to the world or to God. Even if a Christian is temporarily enticed to follow the world, he has the divine power available to him to separate himself from it (cf. 1 John 5:4). If presently your devotion to the world is greater than to God, confess that to Him, and spend time building your faith in Him so that your devotion to Him might increase.

4. Judah had been more than adequately warned about their indifference to God's commandments and their oppression and unrighteousness that would result in judgment (cf. Isa. 5:1-7). Do you remember a time when the Holy Spirit had to warn you several times before you understood His message? Why were you oblivious to the earlier warnings? What finally got your attention? Can you see how God's loving discipline has made you stronger in that particular area? Thank God for His abundant grace and patience as He transforms us from vessels of dishonor to vessels of honor (2 Tim. 2:20-21).

5. Many times in our zeal for God we believe that it is better not to "defile" ourselves by intermingling with nonbelievers. If you have been a Christian for any length of time, you may find that

New American Standard Bible.

you revolve predominantly in Christian circles. What principle was Paul trying to convey to the Corinthians in 1 Corinthians 5:9-11? Do you spend time with your unsaved neighbors? Do you interact with your nonbelieving coworkers? Unbelievers need to see us as salt and light (Matt. 5:13-16). Brainstorm to discover some ways you could befriend unsaved individuals and tell them about Christ. Maybe you could have a neighborhood potluck, or sit next to someone new at lunch, or offer assistance to someone in need.

6. Have you ever been beaten over the head with someone else's conviction? The Pharisees were guilty of doing that. In fact, they even sought to kill Jesus because He challenged their convictions (Mark 3:1-6). The Corinthians had some convictions, too. What does Paul accuse them of lacking as they "ministered" their gifts (1 Cor. 13:1-3)? Have you ever been frustrated with a nonbelieving friend or relative who consistently refused to pursue spiritual things? Have you allowed your approach toward them to be overbearing? What does Paul suggest should be our attitude when communicating with those who oppose us (cf. Rom. 12:14-21; 2 Tim. 2:24-26; Titus 3:1-2)? What instructions does he give with regard to our attitude toward believers regardless of how their convictions may differ from ours (cf. Rom. 12:9-10, 16; Gal. 6:1; 1 Tim. 5:1-2)? If you have fallen short in these areas, pray that God would enable you to manifest the love that His Spirit has "shed abroad in our hearts" (Rom. 5:5; cf. Gal. 5:22-23). We need to be like cups that are filled with love —when someone bumps into us, love spills out onto them.

2

The Consequences of an
Uncompromising Life—Part 1

Outline

Introduction

Lesson
I. An Unashamed Boldness (v. 8)
   A. Illustrated in the Life of Daniel
   B. Illustrated in the Old Testament
      1. By Moses
      2. By David
         a) Psalm 40:8-10
         b) Psalm 71:15
      3. By Daniel's friends
   C. Illustrated in the New Testament
      1. By the exhortation of Jesus
      2. By the encouragement of Peter
      3. By the example of Paul
         a) Acts 24-36
         b) 2 Timothy 1
         c) Philippians 1
II. An Uncommon Standard (v. 12)
   A. Explained
   B. Exemplified
      1. The amorality of wine
      2. The abstinence from wine
III. An Unearthly Protection (v. 9)
   A. The Reason for God's Protection
   B. The Promises of God's Protection

Introduction

Since I began teaching the Word of God, I have believed that where a clear scriptural principle exists, we must always obey it. Some things involve no specific biblical commands. But when we know definitively what the Bible teaches, we must not compromise. Such conviction characterized Daniel. He didn't vacillate on the absolutes of the Word of God. The law was a rock of confidence that allowed him to endure the storms of his opportunity. Of all the young Jewish men deported in 606 B.C., only Daniel and his three friends were able to resist the Chaldeans' brainwashing. Although they chose to accept the education of the Chaldeans, their commitment to God prevented them from being defiled.

The Potential Benefit of Secular Education

Although Christians may be educated in the world's universities and colleges, if their faith in God and their commitment to His Word is strong, then that education will be properly filtered through the Word, enabling them to evaluate the inadequacies of secular theories and theology.

For example, men like Francis Schaeffer who have studied and understood the world's philosophies are better able to answer them with the truth of God. Those scientists who have studied the theories of evolution enable us to intelligently refute them. There are also godly people who have studied the cults and false religions, thus providing resources to counteract false systems and bring the gospel to the people who are trapped in them.

Daniel and his friends didn't fear the Babylonian education because they could filter it through the grid of God's Word. If you expose yourself to those kinds of educational opportunities without that grid, however, you may become shipwrecked in your faith

(1 Tim. 1:19). When people ask if I believe Christians should attend secular universities, I respond that *some* Christians should. Some who are exposed to secular education will learn how to deal with secular philosophies biblically.

Although Daniel accepted the pagan education and name, he abstained from eating the king's food. He refused to adopt the corrupting life-style of the Babylonians. His decision reflected the instruction of Proverbs 4:23, which says, "Keep thy heart with all diligence; for out of it are the issues of life." You must guard your heart, because if you ever give away that part of your being that thinks, responds, and motivates you to action, then the issues of life will be corrupted.

Lesson

Having seen the commitment that characterized Daniel's uncompromising life, we'll look at the consequences of such a commitment. Nebuchadnezzar's plan was to brainwash the Jewish youths. He wanted them to acquire an increasing appetite for the Chaldean culture and forget their Jewish heritage. He wanted them to adopt his life-style. For Daniel to refuse the king's offer could have had serious repercussions. Sometimes a great price must be paid for taking an uncompromising stand. Going against a pagan monarch can be dangerous, but Daniel and his friends did so because they had an uncompromising character. Hananiah, Mishael, and Azariah took a stand and were cast into a fiery furnace (3:16-18, 20). Likewise, Daniel took his stand and was cast into a lions' den (6:10, 16). They refused to compromise.

The text presents the characteristics of one who takes an uncompromising stand. When a person does not compromise in a godless society, he possesses the qualities illustrated in the life of Daniel.

I. AN UNASHAMED BOLDNESS (v. 8)

    A. Illustrated in the Life of Daniel

        "Daniel purposed in his heart that he would not defile himself with the portion of the king's food, nor with the wine which he drank; therefore, he requested of the prince of

the eunuchs [Ashpenaz] that he might not defile himself."
Here is a fascinating example of unashamed boldness.
Daniel was saying that he didn't wish to eat the king's food
or drink the king's wine because it would defile him. That's
a bold statement.

Daniel didn't say that he had to have a special diet. He
didn't try to con the king or the prince of the eunuchs. He
didn't say his body couldn't adjust to such rich food. He
could have made such excuses, but he didn't.

What's Your Excuse?

Too often when we want to escape from a spiritual or moral dilemma, we tend to give a reason other than the biblical one as our excuse not to be involved. We don't want to suggest that others might be wrong. When someone asks us to participate in a sinful activity, we shouldn't be afraid to say, "I believe that is sinful, and I don't want to compromise my commitment to Jesus Christ." Rather, we often say, "That would be enjoyable, but I have to do something else." We sometimes fail to establish the fact that a spiritual issue is at stake.

I love the character of young Daniel. When explaining his
objection, he could have used a word other than *defile*. It's a
strong word; in fact, something that is defiled is an abomination to the Lord (cf. Lev. 18:24-30). The Babylonian food
had been offered to idols and had not been prepared according to Jewish dietary laws. If he violated God's laws,
that would constitute defilement.

In addition, Daniel's reference to defilement implies that
he may have explained to Ashpenaz why it was a defilement. He may have explained the purpose and importance
of Old Testament dietary laws and the commands against
idolatry as well. He refused to eat the food because to do so
would have been contrary to God's law. Isn't it wonderful
when someone in a difficult situation isn't ashamed of being committed to God's Word? That's uncompromising
character. Daniel wasn't ashamed of his faith in God even
in a pagan society where he was a prisoner of the king.
Even the king's right to kill him for disobedience and rebel-

lion never phased his commitment. Proverbs 29:25 says, "The fear of man bringeth a snare." Many Christians are easily intimidated by the fear of man. But not Daniel. Those who have an uncompromising character always seem to have unashamed boldness.

B. Illustrated in the Old Testament

1. By Moses

Moses told Pharaoh, "Let my people go" (Ex. 5:1). That's boldness!

2. By David

a) Psalm 40:8-10

"I delight to do thy will, O my God; yea, thy law is within my heart. I have preached righteousness in the great congregation; lo, I have not restrained my lips, O Lord, thou knowest. I have not hidden thy righteousness within my heart; I have declared thy faithfulness and thy salvation. I have not concealed thy lovingkindness and thy truth from the great congregation" (vv. 9-10). Whenever a person has the law of God in his heart and desires to obey it, he has an uncompromising spirit. David knew God's law and was committed to doing it. He sought never to hold back a word of righteous truth. May God make us people like that!

b) Psalm 71:15

"My mouth shall show forth thy righteousness and thy salvation all the day." David had an unashamed boldness.

3. By Daniel's friends

Daniel 3:13-18 says, "Nebuchadnezzar in his rage and fury commanded to bring Shadrach, Meshach, and Abed-nego. Then they brought these men before the king. Nebuchadnezzar spoke and said unto them, Is it true, O Shadrach, Meshach, and Abed-nego, do not ye

37

serve my gods, nor worship the golden image which I have set up? Now, if ye be ready that at that time that ye hear the sound of the . . . music, to fall down and worship the image which I have made, well; but if ye worship not, ye shall be cast the same hour into the midst of a burning fiery furnace. And who is that God, that shall deliver you out of my hands? Shadrach, Meshach, and Abed-nego answered and said to the king, O Nebuchadnezzar, we are not careful to answer thee in this matter. If it be so, our God, whom we serve, is able to deliver us from the burning fiery furnace, and he will deliver us out of thine hand, O king. But if not, be it known unto thee, O king, that we will not serve thy gods, nor worship the golden image which thou hast set up."

C. Illustrated in the New Testament

1. By the exhortation of Jesus

In Mark 8:38 the Lord says, "Whosoever, therefore, shall be ashamed of me and of my words in this adulterous and sinful generation, of him also shall the Son of man be ashamed, when he cometh in the glory of his Father, with the holy angels." That's a strong statement. Whether the people referred to are actually saved is a debated question. But at times Christians *are* ashamed of Jesus Christ.

2. By the encouragement of Peter

In 1 Peter 4:16 Peter says, "If any man suffer as a Christian, let him not be ashamed." When people ridicule and criticize you for your faith, it's easy to feel ashamed and be afraid to say anything.

3. By the example of Paul

a) Acts 24-36

Near the end of the book of Acts, Paul gave his defense before the Roman rulers Felix, Festus, and

Agrippa. Each time he boldly preached Jesus Christ without hesitation.

b) 2 Timothy 1

Later he sought to instill this boldness in Timothy. He wrote, "God hath not given us the spirit of fear, but of power, and of love, and of a sound mind. Be not thou, therefore, ashamed of the testimony of our Lord, nor of me his prisoner" (vv. 7-8).

c) Philippians 1

Having expressed his earnest hope to be bold (v. 20), Paul said, "Let your conduct be as it becometh the gospel of Christ, that whether I come and see you, or else be absent, I may hear of your affairs, that ye stand fast in one spirit, with one mind striving together for the faith of the gospel; and in nothing terrified by your adversaries" (vv. 27-28). Paul wanted them to boldly stand and speak.

Uncompromising character has a holy, fearless courage that knows no shame in bearing the name of Jesus Christ. Such boldness is the measure of an uncompromising life. Once you purpose to draw the line wherever God draws it, you will have, like Daniel, the boldness to speak His Word before kings. And that's the kind of person God uses.

II. AN UNCOMMON STANDARD (v. 12)

A. Explained

People who have an uncompromising life don't live the way everyone else does. They will inevitably have an uncommon standard. They set their standard above the masses, even above that of the average Christian. When I was in high school I read about people who were devoutly committed to praying. I also read the biographies of missionaries who did not live the Christian life the same way as people I knew. They lived on an entirely different level. That uncommon standard was expressed in the life of Daniel.

Daniel in effect said, "I don't want any portion of the king's food or wine." Daniel requests a special diet in verse 12: "Let them give us vegetables to eat, and water to drink." Although Daniel could not drink the wine and eat the food of the king, he could have had something other than vegetables and water. But he wanted to maintain an uncommon standard. Instead of the king's meat and wine, he chose to drink only water and eat pulse—a mixture of beans and seeds.

People who make the commitment Daniel made desire to live on the highest plane. Their ministries are a cut above the rest because they have a higher level of commitment. They have a more faithful prayer life and a greater commitment to the study of the Word.

B. Exemplified

1. The amorality of wine

Why did Daniel refuse to drink any wine for the entire three years of conditioning when it wasn't required of him? The Old Testament speaks of wine (Heb., *yayin*) as a common part of Jewish society. I believe that when wine was diluted with water, it was considered proper to drink.

a) Exodus 29:40 says that wine was used in the drink offering of the sacrificial system.

b) First Chronicles 9:29 says that a supply of wine was kept in the Temple.

c) Isaiah 24:9 associates drinking wine with singing and being joyful.

d) Isaiah 55:1-2 identifies wine as a symbol of salvation.

In the Old Testament we see that properly mixed wine was not evil in itself.

2. The abstinence from wine

   a) By the priests (Lev. 10:8-11)

   The Lord set this standard for Aaron, the high priest, and the other serving priests: "The Lord spoke unto Aaron, saying, Do not drink wine [Heb., *yayin*] nor strong drink [Heb., *shekar*], thou, nor thy sons with thee, when ye go into the tabernacle of the congregation, lest ye die: it shall be a statute forever throughout your generations; and that ye may put difference between holy and unholy, and between unclean and clean; and that ye may teach the children of Israel all the statutes which the Lord hath spoken unto them by the hand of Moses." If the priests drank wine or strong drink while ministering, they might have lost the ability to distinguish the holy from the unholy, and to rightly teach the people. Therefore total abstinence was required of a functioning priest.

   b) By the Nazirites (Num. 6:1-4)

   "The Lord spoke unto Moses, saying, Speak unto the children of Israel, and say unto them, When either man or woman shall separate themselves to vow a vow of a Nazirite [meaning "to be separated"], to separate themselves unto the Lord; he shall separate himself from wine and strong drink, and shall drink no vinegar of wine, or vinegar of strong drink, neither shall he drink any liquor of grapes, nor eat moist grapes, or dried. All the days of his separation shall he eat nothing that is made of the vine tree, from the kernels even to the husk." Everyone wasn't required to live that way. Only those who wanted to live uniquely separated unto God chose such an uncommon standard.

   c) By the Rechabites (Jer. 35:5-7)

   "I set before the sons of the house of Rechabites pots full of wine, and cups, and I said unto them, Drink

wine. But they said, We will drink no wine; for Jona-
dab, the son of Rechab, our father, commanded us,
saying, Ye shall drink no wine, neither ye, nor your
sons forever; neither shall ye build house, nor sow
seed, nor plant vineyard, nor have any, but all your
days ye shall dwell in tents, that ye may live many
days in the land where ye be sojourners." The Rechabites, out of a personal commitment to God, were assigned an uncommon standard. They took a place
above the crowd.

d) By rulers (Prov. 31:4-6)

"It is not for kings, O Lemuel, it is not for kings to
drink wine, nor for princes strong drink" (v. 4). Daniel may have come from a royal family and been
taught that important principle. Verse 5 states that
rulers should abstain from drinking "lest they drink,
and forget the law, and pervert the justice of any of
the afflicted. Give strong drink unto him that is ready
to perish" (vv. 5-6). When someone was near death,
he could be sedated with wine, but is was not to be
consumed by those who had to make important spiritual decisions. Those with the greatest spiritual responsibility should always uphold an uncommon
standard.

e) By Timothy (1 Tim. 5:23)

The apostle Paul told Timothy, "Drink no longer water, but use a little wine for thy stomach's sake and
thy frequent infirmities." I believe Paul instructed
Timothy in this way because Timothy never drank
anything but water. Although drinking wine was not
specifically prohibited, apparently Timothy chose to
abstain and set an uncommon standard.

f) By John the Baptist (Luke 1:15)

Of John the Baptist an angel said, "He shall be great
in the sight of the Lord, and shall drink neither wine
nor strong drink."

g) By the elders (Titus 1:7)

One qualification that Paul gave for an elder was that he be "not given to wine."

Those who desire to live at the most uncompromising level of commitment establish an uncommon standard. Wanting to be distinguished from the gluttons and drunkards of Babylon, Daniel refused to drink not only the king's wine, but any wine at all. Although refusing to drink wine doesn't make a believer more spiritual, it's one place where he can set an uncommon standard.

The Course of History Affected by Wine

Great men have fallen to the power of drink. In Daniel 5, Belteshazzar lost the Babylonian Empire while in a drunken stupor. History records that Alexander the Great lost his world empire at the age of thirty-three partly because of wine.

Commentator W. A. Criswell notes how wine played an integral part in the defeat of two French armies: "When the Iron Duke of England, Wellington, was marching his army across the Iberian peninsula, word was brought to his headquarters that ahead of him was a vast store of Spanish wine. He stopped his army. He sent some of his men ahead and they blew it up. Then he marched his army on. It is said that the reason Napoleon Bonaparte lost the battle of Waterloo to the victorious Duke of Wellington was because the night before Marshall Ney tarried too long over his favorite glass of wine and the next morning his head was clouded and his mind unsteady. When France fell in World War II against Hitler, Marshall Petain said, 'France was defeated because its army was drunk.' And the Vichy government of 1940 said the reason for the collapse of the moral fiber of the French army was due to alcohol" (*Expository Sermons on the Book of Daniel* [Grand Rapids, Mich.: Zondervan, n.d.], p. 37).

An uncompromising life like Daniel's doesn't play on the edge of what is right, but rather chooses the highest, the noblest, and the best.

III. AN UNEARTHLY PROTECTION (v. 9)

In verse 8 "Daniel purposed in his heart," and in verse 9 "God . . . brought Daniel into favor and compassion with the prince of the eunuchs." God responds to that kind of commitment.

A. The Reason for God's Protection

What caused Ashpenaz to look with favor upon Daniel? Two possibilities exist. First, even people who disagree with your convictions usually admire you for keeping them. People don't respect cowardly individuals who vacillate. People respect individuals with strong moral convictions.

But I don't believe Daniel's integrity swayed Ashpenaz, the prince of the eunuchs. It is true that Daniel had a gracious and loving personality. That is evident from the way he spoke (vv. 11-13). But the real reason Ashpenaz favored Daniel was the sovereignty of God. Verse 9 says, "God had brought Daniel into favor and compassion." God controls everything. He had a purpose for Daniel: He wanted him to be a witness in Babylon. I believe Daniel's influence was responsible for the wise men who came from the East centuries later at the birth of Christ. Behind the return of the Jews to their land after seventy years of captivity was Daniel, serving as the agent of God. Therefore God sovereignly caused Ashpenaz to have favor and compassion upon Daniel. Even Nebuchadnezzar couldn't change the plan of God.

When we live uncompromising lives, we will experience supernatural protection. People who are afraid to speak out for truth sometimes say to me, "When you teach what you believe the Bible says, don't you worry about what could happen?" Any worry is only temporary because I believe that until God is finished with me, He will protect me. God protects those who are committed to Him. Usually we are tempted to compromise when we're afraid of the consequences of standing for truth. But if we didn't compromise, God would protect us in trouble. As soon as we compromise truth, we forfeit that protection. And one compromise leads to another until we become trapped.

B. The Promises of God's Protection

Several verses illustrate God's bringing one into favor with his enemies.

1. 1 Kings 8:50—"Forgive thy people who have sinned against thee, and all their transgressions in which they have transgressed against thee, and give them compassion before them who carried them captive, that they may have compassion on them." Solomon requested that God allow Israel's captors to be compassionate should Israel be taken into captivity. And God did.

Would You Compromise Under Persecution?

People sometimes ask, "If we lived in a society that persecuted us for our faith, would we still speak the truth?" If we compromised, we would be on our own. But if we spoke the truth, God would be our protector. If God wants you to live, no king in the world can take your life. You would have nothing to fear. You might say, "If I stand for truth, I'll lose my job!" But if you compromise, you'll lose God's resource! Whose support do you want, your boss's or God's? No boss in the world can move you until God allows it.

2. Psalm 106:46—God cares so much for His people Israel that "he made them also to be pitied of all those that carried them captives." God didn't work only on Ashpenaz's heart; He made all the Babylonians compassionate toward His people. God can sway not only a king but an entire society as well. He did so because "he remembered for them his covenant" (v. 45). As Christians, we have a covenant with God in Christ. If we live an uncompromising life, God will take care of us.

3. Proverbs 16:7—"When a man's ways please the Lord, he maketh even his enemies to be at peace with him."

The point of life is to please the Lord. Therefore live with unashamed boldness and an uncommon standard, and gain an unearthly protection.

Conclusion

People's hearts are in the hands of God. Our responsibility is to please God and allow Him control of people's hearts. Daniel's life portrays what God does for those who are faithfully obedient to Him. Verse 9 records that God caused Ashpenaz to feel "favor and compassion" toward Daniel. The Hebrew word translated "favor" means "bowels of compassion"—a gut-level affection. "Compassion" speaks of a tender, unfailing love. Ashpenaz loved Daniel. God was accomplishing His plan for Daniel.

The application is clear: If you want to accomplish something in God's kingdom, don't compromise. Allow God to place you where He wants. If He wants to lift you up in a society, a church, a ministry, or some other situation, He will change the hearts of those in authority as you live an uncompromising life. Don't seek your own advancement. God will take special care of His faithful, uncompromising people. Moses was placed among the reeds of the Nile (Ex. 2:3). But soon he was living in Pharaoh's palace, because Pharaoh's daughter found him and adopted him as her own (vv. 5-10). And his own mother nursed him. Who masterminded that? God. We don't need to use politics or self-effort to accomplish God's purposes. We must live uncompromising lives and trust God's sovereign power.

Focusing on the Facts

1. What prevented Daniel and his three friends from being defiled by Chaldean education? Explain (see pp. 34-35).
2. What is the potential benefit of secular education (see pp. 34-35)?
3. What price did Daniel and his friends have to pay for taking an uncompromising stand (Dan. 3:20; 6:16; see p. 35)?
4. Explain how Daniel demonstrated unashamed boldness before Ashpenaz (see pp. 35-36).
5. How did David express his boldness in Psalms 40:8-10 and 71:15 (see p. 37)?
6. What phrase in Daniel 3:17-18 shows that Daniel's three friends fully trusted God? Which verse shows that they were willing to suffer the consequences (see p. 38)?

7. What quality can be used to measure whether we are living an uncompromising life (see p. 39)?
8. What kind of people does God use (see p. 39)?
9. What type of standard do those with uncompromising lives have? Explain (see p. 39).
10. The Old Testament talks about wine as a _____ _____ of Jewish society. When was wine considered proper to drink (see p. 40)?
11. Why was total abstinence required of a functioning priest (see p. 41)? Why were kings to abstain from drinking (Prov. 31:5; see p. 42)?
12. What indicates that Timothy drank only water (see p. 42)?
13. What was the real reason for Ashpenaz's positive attitude toward Daniel (see pp. 43-44)?
14. What two historic events did Daniel apparently influence (see p. 44)?
15. When do we forfeit God's protection (see p. 44)?

Pondering the Principles

1. Read Proverbs 4:23. Why is it important to "keep [one's] heart with all diligence" (see p. 34)? How are you guarding your heart? Are you allowing the world's system to influence you more than God's truth? Paul exhorts us to "be alert and sober" (1 Thess. 5:6, NASB), since we are "sons of light" (v. 5). What protects our hearts from being saturated with the doubt and indifference of the world? Your faith in God can grow through prayer and Bible study and by acting upon that faith with expressions of love (v. 8). Memorize Proverbs 4:23, and begin practicing its truth today.

2. God was ultimately responsible for sovereignly changing Ashpenaz's heart. But God used Daniel's integrity to establish his credibility. If we talk to unbelievers about how God changes lives, but no changes are evident in us, God cannot use us to influence them for Christ. Read 1 Peter 1:11-17. What two things mentioned in verse 15 cause unbelievers to glorify God as He visits them with salvation? If anything in your life would prevent your relatives or friends from glorifying God, confess it to God and submit yourself to the control of His Spirit.

3. Since the hearts of all people are in the hand of God, who is responsible to convert the unbeliever? According to 1 Peter 3:15-16, what is our responsibility? Does that relieve any guilt you feel about those who rejected the gospel you proclaimed? Realize that although we are responsible for proclaiming the truth, God is responsible for changing people's hearts.

3

The Consequences of an
Uncompromising Life—Part 2

Outline

Introduction
A. Examples of Compromise
B. Examples of Commitment

Review
I. An Unashamed Boldness (v. 8)
II. An Uncommon Standard (v. 12)
III. An Unearthly Protection (v. 9)
  A. The Reason for God's Protection
  B. The Promise of God's Protection

Lesson
IV. An Unhindered Persistence (vv. 10-11)
  A. The Dilemma of Ashpenaz (v. 10)
  B. The Determination of Daniel (v. 11)
    1. Explained
    2. Illustrated
V. An Unblemished Faith (vv. 12-13)
  A. The Principle Explained
  B. The Principle Enacted
VI. An Unusual Test (vv. 14-16)
  A. The Steward's Evaluation (v. 14)
  B. God's Intervention (vv. 15-16)
    1. Passing the test (v. 15)
    2. Avoiding the defilement (v. 16)
VII. An Unmeasurable Blessing (vv. 18-20)
  A. The Benefits of God's Blessing (v. 17)
    1. To all the youths (v. 17a)
    2. To Daniel (v. 17b)

Introduction

Someone once said, "Every man has his price." Your price is the point at which your would abandon your moral standards for personal gain.

Does every person have a price? Do all of us have moral standards that are valid only as long as they accommodate our desires? Or do we set aside our desires for the sake of those standards we say we believe? People throughout history have refused to compromise. Martin Luther stood before the Diet of Worms, who demanded that he recant his writings or lose his life. But he did not deny Christ. Hugh Latimer and Nicholas Ridley, two English reformers, were both burned at the stake for their faith in Christ. People such as those men have no price—they can't be bought.

However, we often hear of people who boast of their moral standards and extol their righteous character, yet abandon their convictions when compromise is more beneficial.

What Are the Limits of Your Convictions?

- Sometimes people say they believe the Bible but stay in churches where the Bible isn't taught.
- Sometimes people affirm that sin must be punished until those sins are committed by their children.
- Sometimes people say one must speak out against dishonesty and corruption until they have to confront their bosses and face losing their jobs.
- Sometimes people have high moral standards until their lusts are kindled by unscriptural relationships.

- Sometimes people are honest until a little dishonesty will save them money.
- Sometimes people know something is definitely wrong, but for the sake of maintaining peace they cover up the truth.
- Sometimes people claim to hold a conviction but violate it if it is challenged by someone they admire or fear.
- Sometimes people know what ought to be said but don't say it because they believe they might lose face.

A. Examples of Compromise

1. Adam compromised God's law, followed his wife's sin, and lost paradise (Gen. 3:6, 22-24).

2. Abraham compromised the truth, lied about Sarah, and nearly lost his wife (Gen. 12:10-20).

3. Sarah compromised God's Word and sent Abraham to Hagar, who bore Ishmael and destroyed peace in the Middle East (Gen. 16:1-4, 11-12).

4. Esau compromised for a meal Jacob prepared and lost his birthright (Gen. 25:29-34).

5. Saul compromised God's divine Word, kept the animals, and lost his kingdom (1 Sam. 15:3, 20-28).

6. Aaron compromised, and he and the people lost the privilege of entering the Promised Land (Num. 20:24; cf. Ps. 95:8-11).

7. Samson compromised his devotion as a Nazirite and lost his strength, his eyes, and his life (Judg. 16:4-6, 16-31).

8. Israel compromised the commands of the Lord, lived in sin, and when fighting the Philistines, lost the Ark of God (1 Sam. 4:1-11).

9. David compromised the standard of God, committed adultery with Bathsheba, murdered Uriah, and lost his infant son (2 Sam. 11:1–12:23).

10. Solomon compromised his convictions, married foreign wives, and lost the united kingdom (1 Kings 11:1-8).

11. Ahab compromised, married Jezebel, and lost his throne (1 Kings 16:30-33; 21:1-19; 22:34-38).

12. Israel compromised the law of God with sin and idolatry and lost her homeland (2 Chron. 36:14-17).

13. Peter compromised his conviction about Christ, denied Him, and lost his joy. Later he compromised the truth for acceptance by the Judaizers and lost his liberty (Mark 14:66-72; Gal. 2:11-14).

14. Ananias and Sapphira compromised their word about giving, lied to the Holy Spirit, and lost their lives (Acts 5:1-11).

15. For thirty pieces of silver Judas compromised his supposed devotion to Christ and was separated from Christ eternally (Matt. 26:20-25, 47-49; 27:1-5; cf. John 17:12).

B. Examples of Commitment

In contrast, several individuals have shown that they couldn't be bought off: Moses before Pharaoh; David on several different occasions; Paul before Festus, Felix, and Agrippa; and Daniel before Nebuchadnezzar. Daniel 1:8 says, "Daniel purposed in his heart that he would not defile himself with the portion of the king's food, nor with the wine which he drank; therefore, he requested of the prince of the eunuchs that he might not defile himself." No better biblical illustration of an undefiled, uncompromising man exists than Daniel. During the seventy years that he lived in Babylon with the pagan Chaldeans, he never compromised his convictions.

Review

After besieging Jerusalem, the Babylonians captured as many as seventy-five Jewish youths to train them to rule over Jewish affairs. The young men were provided Babylonian education, names, and food. But Daniel and his three friends refused the king's food so they would not violate God's Word. Because they stood firm while the other young men gave in, Daniel and his friends are a tremendous illustration of conviction.

The Conviction of the Cadets

Such conviction is expressed in the "Cadet Prayer," repeated in chapel services by the cadets at West Point. Part of the prayer says, "Make us choose the harder right instead of the easier wrong, and never to be content with a half truth when the whole can be won. Endow us with courage that is born of loyalty to all that is noble and worthy, that scorns to compromise with vice and injustice and knows no fear when right and truth are in jeopardy."

The Price of Compromise

Aesop understood the price of compromise. He speaks in his fable "The Bat" about a time when the beasts and the fowls were engaged in war. The bat tried to pacify both sides. When the birds were victorious, he said that he was a bird; when the beasts won, he assured them that he was a beast. But soon his hypocrisy was discovered, and he was rejected by both the beasts and the birds. Consequently he had to hide all day and could appear only at night (*Aesop Without Morals* [New York: Thomas Yoseloff, 1961], p. 257).

We have examined three characteristics of an uncompromising life.

I. AN UNASHAMED BOLDNESS (v. 8; see pp. 35-39)

II. AN UNCOMMON STANDARD (v. 12; see pp. 39-43)

Those who have great spiritual responsibility should have an uncommon standard. An uncompromising life doesn't play on the edge of the acceptable; it chooses the highest and noblest standard of all, regardless of the price.

The Flying Scotsman

For months Eric Liddell trained for the 100-meter race in the 1924 Paris Olympics. Sportswriters all over the country predicted that Liddell would win. Then Liddell learned that the 100-meter race was scheduled for Sunday. He believed that he would not honor God by competing on the Lord's Day and refused to race. His fans were stunned. Some who had previously praised him called him a fool. But Eric stood firm. He asked to train for the 400-meter race, scheduled for a weekday, even though it was four times longer. Liddell not only won, but he also set a world record. God honored his uncompromising spirit. Later Eric Liddell went to China as a missionary where, in 1945, he died in a war camp. He was uncompromising even in death. (Liddell's story is told in Sally Magnusson's *The Flying Scotsman* [New York: Quartet, 1981]).

III. AN UNEARTHLY PROTECTION (v. 9; see pp. 43-46)

A. The Reason for God's Protection (see p. 44)

God controls every living being. He can protect those who refuse to compromise. To be uncompromising is to invite God's protection; but to compromise is to eliminate divine protection and possibly bring judgment.

B. The Promise of God's Protection (see pp. 44-46)

Is God Your Defender or Judge?

First Samuel 2:22-25 says, "Eli was very old, and heard all that his sons did unto all Israel, and how they lay with the women who assembled at the door of the tabernacle of the congregation. And he said unto them, Why do ye such things? For I hear of your evil dealings by all this people. Nay, my sons; for it is no good report that I hear: ye make the Lord's people to transgress. If one man sin against another, the judge shall judge him; but if a man sin against the Lord, who shall mediate for him? Notwithstanding, they hearkened not unto the voice of their father, because the Lord would slay them." God kept them in a constant state of rebellion so that He could judge them, because they had gone beyond the possibility of repenting (cf. Ex. 7:3-5; Josh. 11:20). In verse 30, a prophet pronounces judgment: "Wherefore the Lord God of Israel saith, I said indeed that thy house, and the house of thy father should walk before me forever; but now the Lord saith, Be it far from me; for them who honor me I will honor, and they who despise me shall be lightly esteemed." God was telling Eli that although he was the high priest and had all the promises of that priesthood, he would lose them because he dishonored God by putting his sons above Him. The way we live either brings God to our defense or sets Him against us.

Joseph and Daniel are almost parallel in their circumstances. After being sold into slavery by his evil brothers, Joseph eventually became prime minister of Egypt. Both Joseph and Daniel served in a foreign kingdom as prime ministers. Both possessed extraordinary prophetic powers that elevated them to leadership. And both were able to confound the pretenders and phonies in those kingdoms. In spite of the satanic charlatans swarming the courts of Egypt and Babylon, these two men were protected by God and given places of prominence because of their uncompromising lives.

People who live uncompromising lives will often be elevated by God. Someone once said that politics is the art of compromise, that no one can reach a high place in politics without compromising. However, if God wants you there, He'll put you there. But if you compromise to reach that place, you'll find yourself there on your own. Compromise removes us from the place of protection.

Lesson

IV. AN UNHINDERED PERSISTENCE (vv. 10-11)

A. The Dilemma of Ashpenaz (v. 10)

"The prince of the eunuchs said unto Daniel, I fear my lord, the king, who hath appointed your food and your drink; for why should he see your faces worse looking than the youths who are of your age? Then shall ye make me endanger my head with the king."

It's interesting that Ashpenaz gives Daniel the reason. That shows he did have compassion. As much as he liked Daniel and his friends, Ashpenaz didn't want to risk losing his life should they appear "worse looking" ("pale" or "wan," a sign of inadequate nourishment).

B. The Determination of Daniel (v. 11)

1. Explained

Without being cantankerous or pushy, Daniel diplomatically pursues another alternative: "Then said Daniel to Melzar" (v. 11). Because the Hebrew definite article appears before "Melzar," it should probably be understood as meaning "steward" rather than understood as a proper name. As the prince of the eunuchs, Ashpenaz, who was responsible for all the young men in the courts, appointed certain stewards to guard them. The steward of verse 11 was apparently assigned to Daniel and his friends.

After failing to receive the answer he wanted from Ashpenaz, Daniel appealed to a steward, whom Ashpenaz had personally set "over Daniel, Hananiah, Mishael, and Azariah" (v. 11). It was to him that Daniel went with an undaunted spirit.

Some people say, "I know what was right, but I tried to do it and it didn't work out, so I had to go along with what the others were doing." Others superficial-

56

ly exhaust a few resources, then say, "I gave it my best try, but it didn't work out." An uncompromising character, however, never gives up.

2. Illustrated

On the way to Jerusalem, Paul was informed that trouble awaited him. The prophet Agabus took Paul's belt and tied up his own hands and feet as an illustration of what would happen to him when he reached Jerusalem (Acts 21:10-11). Yet Paul already knew that. In Acts 20:23-24 he says, "The Holy Spirit witnesseth in every city, saying that bonds and afflictions await me. But none of these things move me, neither count I my life dear unto myself, so that I might finish my course with joy, and the ministry, which I have received of the Lord Jesus" (Acts 20:23-24).

Daniel had a similar attitude. Just because Ashpenaz shut the door didn't mean Daniel was finished. He had an unhindered persistence. An uncompromising life keeps going until the goal is reached. It won't compromise or quit.

V. AN UNBLEMISHED FAITH (vv. 12-13)

A. The Principle Explained

Daniel believed God would make his request possible. How did he develop that confidence? As a basic spiritual principle, sin brings doubt, and purity brings confidence. When a person is living a holy life, he has a sense of invincibility that believes God will deliver. Daniel had that kind of unblemished faith.

Like Daniel, we can endure any trial without fear when our hearts are pure. Romans 8:31 says, "If God be for us, who can be against us?" In Isaiah 43:2, 5 the Lord promises Israel, "When thou passest through the waters, I will be with thee; when thou walkest through the fire, thou shalt not be burned, neither shall the flame kindle upon thee. . . . Fear not; for I am with thee." When a heart is pure, an unblemished faith remains.

B. The Principle Enacted

Daniel proposed, "Test thy servants, I beseech thee, ten days, and let them give us vegetables to eat, and water to drink. Then let our countenances be looked upon before thee, and the countenance of the youths that eat of the portion of the king's food; and as thou seest, deal with thy servants" (vv. 12-13). That is the confident faith that develops in an uncompromising spirit.

Daniel's faith sprang from a pure heart. Although he had been through a terrible disaster, and many people, like Habakkuk, believed that God had abandoned Judah, Daniel firmly believed that God would respond. Ten days of vegetables compared to ten days of the king's food wouldn't make much difference physiologically. But Daniel was counting on divine intervention. I believe God revealed that test to Daniel because of Daniel's confidence and the Lord's response (vv. 9, 17). Daniel essentially said, "I'll take a stand, and God will honor my uncompromising spirit." That's unblemished faith.

If you live an uncompromising life—regardless of who becomes angry or how many are offended because of what they term a lack of love—God will honor it. If you stand against sin and evil, God will fill your life with joy and happiness. If you stand with honesty, God will sustain and support you. If you truly believe those things, you won't compromise—you'll take God at His word.

VI. AN UNUSUAL TEST (vv. 14-16)

A. The Steward's Evaluation (v. 14)

"He consented to them in this matter, and tested them ten days."

All commitment will be tested. James 1:2-3 speaks of trials that test our faith. The reality of our faith is proven when it's tested. When Daniel decided to stake his faith on God's Word, immediately he was tested.

B. God's Intervention (vv. 15-16)

1. Passing the test (v. 15)

"At the end of ten days, their countenances appeared fairer and fatter in flesh [their appearance had signs of health and vigor] than all the youths who did eat the portion of the king's food."

That had to be the intervention of God because normally in ten days a noticeable change in a person's physiology would not occur.

2. Avoiding the defilement (v. 16)

"Thus Melzar took away the portion of their food, and the wine that they should drink, and gave them vegetables."

God must have intervened because the steward was easily convinced. It may be that he ate the king's food himself for the next three years, which was more than a fair exchange for him. But he gave vegetables and water to Daniel and his three friends, whose uncompromising spirits God honored. They had won the battle by avoiding the life-style the Chaldeans wanted to impose upon them.

VII. AN UNMEASURABLE BLESSING (vv. 18-20)

A. The Benefits of God's Blessing (v. 17)

"As for these four youths, God gave them knowledge and skill in all learning and wisdom; and Daniel had understanding in all visions and dreams."

This is a tremendous illustration of two truths working together: God's sovereign blessing and man's total commitment. God sovereignly blessed them when they were totally committed to live an uncompromising life. From the human perspective, their success depended upon their commitment. But from God's perspective, everything was entirely in His control. Those two concepts are inseparably bound together.

1. To all the youths (v. 17a)

   "Knowledge and skill in all learning and wisdom."

   God taught all four what they needed to know for productive, godly living in Babylonian society. Babylon was the center of learning in its day. It had advanced sciences, comprehensive libraries, and great scholars. But God gave them not only the ability to absorb that knowledge but also the wisdom to apply His Word to their circumstances.

2. To Daniel (v. 17b)

   "Understanding in all visions and dreams."

   God enabled Daniel to interpret dreams and to receive visions. Visions and dreams were both means of revelation from God—the former occurred while the prophet was awake and the latter while he was asleep. Therefore Daniel was a vehicle of God's divine revelations. Verse 17, then, becomes the backdrop for the rest of Daniel's prophecy.

B. The Outcome of God's Blessing (vv. 18-20)

   1. Their success (vv. 18-19b)

      "At the end of the days that the king had said he should bring them in [after the three years of training], then the prince of the eunuchs brought them in before Nebuchadnezzar. And the king conversed with them, and among them all was found none like Daniel, Hananiah, Mishael, and Azariah."

      Having completed their training, all the young men deported in 606 B.C. were personally examined by the king, "and among them all was found none like Daniel, Hananiah, Mishael, and Azariah" (v. 19). Like those four, you can live a life that is so pure, righteous, and full of character that even the world has to acknowledge its quality.

2. Their service (v. 19c)

"Therefore stood they before the king."

Those four young men became the king's personal servants. Imagine standing alongside the king in the royal court of a foreign nation, having been lifted by God to that place at the age of seventeen or eighteen. Without compromising, Daniel ruled in Babylon as prime minister for seventy years (Dan. 2:48; cf. 6:1-2).

3. Their superiority (v. 20)

"In all matters of wisdom and understanding that the king inquired of them, he found them ten times better than all the magicians and astrologers that were in all his realm."

As Christians we have the revelation of God and the indwelling Spirit, so we are far wiser than a genius who doesn't know God. Knowing that, let God lift you up. If someone threatens to force you to compromise, remain true to the Word of God. Don't allow anyone to intimidate you into watering down the absolute, inviolable truth of God. Hold your convictions with the same love and graciousness that Daniel did, but never compromise. And God will honor you and set you above those who are esteemed as the best in your circle of influence.

VIII. AN UNLIMITED INFLUENCE (v. 21)

"Daniel continued even unto the first year of King Cyrus."

Daniel served in an influential position for seventy years. His integrity and uncompromising character had far-reaching results. God gave him the influence that led to the decree of Cyrus to send the Israelites back to their land; influence that led to the rebuilding of the wall under Nehemiah and the reestablishing of the nation of Israel; influence that eventually led the wise men to crown the King who was born in Bethlehem. Daniel was behind the scenes of the history of the Messiah as well as the Messiah's people. His prophecy glorifies the "KING OF KINGS, AND LORD OF LORDS" (Rev. 19:16) who reigns forever.

Conclusion

An uncompromising life is characterized by an unashamed boldness that calls us to an uncommon standard. It depends on an unearthly protection, as we demonstrate an unblemished faith, for which we face unusual tests with an unhindered persistence. Then God brings unmeasurable blessings and unlimited influence.

Don't compromise. Allow God to do with your life as He pleases, that He may broaden your influence and glorify Himself.

Focusing on the Facts

1. Why do people often abandon their convictions (see pp. 50-51)?
2. Give some biblical examples of people who compromised (see pp. 51-52).
3. Why did Esau and Peter compromise (see pp. 51-52)?
4. Who is one of the best illustrations of an uncompromising life? Explain (see p. 52).
5. How was Eric Liddell an example of unswerving commitment (see pp. 53-54)?
6. What can result from continual compromise (1 Sam. 2:22-25, 30; 4:11; see pp. 54-55)?
7. How are Joseph and Daniel similar (see p. 55)?
8. Why didn't Ashpenaz honor Daniel's request (see p. 55)?
9. How did Daniel pursue his goal (see p. 56)?
10. As a basic spiritual principle, _____ brings doubt and _____ brings confidence (see p. 57).
11. Because eating vegetables for ten days wouldn't make much physiological difference, Daniel must have been counting on what (see p. 57)?
12. When is the reality of our faith proven (see p. 58)?
13. What extra blessing did Daniel receive? Explain (see p. 59).

14. How did Daniel and his three friends compare with the other Jewish youths being evaluated by the king and the Babylonian soothsayers (Dan. 1:19-20; see p. 60)?

Pondering the Principles

1. Although many Christians don't agree completely with Eric Liddell's interpretation of the Sabbath, we can still respect him for his commitment to his conviction. He was fully persuaded that he could not honor God by running on Sunday. Read Romans 14:5-14. Does that passage indicate that believers will have differing convictions? According to Romans 14, if someone makes a commitment believing he is honoring the Lord, should we condemn his belief if we disagree? Why? Have others criticized you for your convictions? Did you hold them in love without criticizing others who disagree with you? Ask God to give you the boldness to stand for what you believe Scripture teaches and the love to accept those who disagree.

2. Why was Paul willing to suffer the "bonds and afflictions" that awaited him in Jerusalem (see Acts 20:23-24)? Have you been called to a ministry that, from a human perspective, is a thankless job? Are you willing to sacrifice whatever is necessary to see that ministry successfully completed? Are you experiencing the joy that goes with such committed service? If not, take time now to evaluate your motivations for ministering.

3. What did sin do to David's confidence before God (see Psalm 51:1-12)? Do you sense a lack of confidence in God? Is it because some impurity in your life hasn't been cleansed? Sin not only brings doubt, but fear of divine discipline and a loss of joy as well (Ps. 51:11-12). If sin has destroyed your confidence in God, make Psalm 51:7-10 your prayer.

4

Uncompromising Faith in the Fiery Furnace—Part 1

Outline

Introduction
A. Worshiping the Wrong God
   1. Scripture on idolatry
      a) Explained
      b) Illustrated
      c) Denounced
         (1) Romans 1
         (2) Exodus 20
      d) Examined
         (1) Manifestations of idolatry
         (2) Condemnations of idolatry
         (3) Consequences of idolatry
         (4) Judgments on idolatry
   2. Idolatry in society
B. Worshiping the Right God in the Wrong Way
   1. Explained
   2. Illustrated
      a) In the history of the church
      b) In the history of Israel
         (1) The provision of salvation
         (2) The perversion of the serpent

Lesson
I. The Ceremony (vv. 1-3)
   A. The Act of Idolatry (v. 1)
      1. The image
         a) Its dimensions
         b) Its construction
         c) Its location

2. The intentions
   a) Unifying the nation
   b) Verifying loyalty
   c) Preventing factions
   d) Glorifying self
B. The Acceptance of the Invitation (vv. 2-3)
   1. The recipients (v. 2)
   2. The subtle repetition (v. 3)

Introduction

A. Worshiping the Wrong God

I once read about a religious man who purchased a statue of Christ for his home. He set it on the coffee table in his living room, but his wife didn't believe it complemented the room's decor, so she moved it to the den. Later the husband moved it to another area of the house, which finally prompted their child to ask, "Can't you decide what to do with God?"

That is precisely the issue in Daniel 3. It separates those who didn't put God in His rightful place from three who did. A theme throughout Scripture is the conflict between those who give God the respect due Him and those who do not.

1. Scripture on idolatry

People are incurably religious. All races and ethnic groups have some religion. People inevitably bow at some shrine. They may worship the true God or some false substitute, but they will worship.

a) Explained

Romans 1:21 says that when men "knew God, they glorified him not as God." Then man began to worship the creature more than the Creator. He began to worship man, birds, beasts, and creeping things. Therefore Romans 1 makes clear that when a man rejects the true God, he doesn't enter a religious vacuum: he will worship the creature if he doesn't worship the Creator.

The Old Testament teaches that man characteristically creates a god like himself and then becomes like that god. By doing that, he accommodates his sinfulness, because one difficulty in worshiping the true God is having to face our inadequacy and sinfulness. A god like us is much easier to live with than a holy God.

Psalm 115 gives us insight into that process. Verses 1-8 say, "Not unto us, O Lord, not unto us, but unto thy name give glory, for thy mercy, and for thy truth's sake. Wherefore should the nations say, Where is now their God? But our God is in the heavens; he hath done whatsoever he hath pleased. Their idols are silver and gold, the work of men's hands. They have mouths, but they speak not; eyes have they, but they see not. They have ears, but they hear not; noses have they, but they smell not. They have hands, but they handle not; feet have they, but they walk not; neither speak they through their throat. They who make them are like unto them; so is everyone who trusteth in them" (vv. 1-8). The Bible says that "God created man in his own image" (Gen. 1:27). But man creates gods in his image—the ultimate form of rebellion. Therefore continual conflict exists between the worship of the true God and the worship of gods fashioned by the imagination of men.

b) Illustrated

The Old Testament repeatedly mentions a god known as Baal, a title which simply means "lord." The Canaanites believed that Baal was the force behind sexual relations between a man and a woman. Therefore, any sexual act became an expression of the power of Baal and a sacred act. The temples of Baal were occupied by priestesses known as sacred prostitutes. They were considered to be holy women; to have intercourse with them was believed to unite one with Baal.

Man invents gods that accommodate his vile sinfulness. Inevitably, those gods lead people into immorality because they reflect the sinfulness of the people who invented them.

c) Denounced

(1) Romans 1

When men knew God, they glorified Him not as God, and they changed the glory of God into an image (vv. 21, 23). As a result, "God also gave them up to uncleanness through the lusts of their own hearts, to dishonor their own bodies between themselves" (v. 24). The rejection of the true God occurs in verse 21, the establishment of false gods occurs in verses 22-23, and the consequent immorality occurs in verse 24.

(2) Exodus 20

In the first two of the Ten Commandments, the Lord said, "Thou shalt have no other gods before me. Thou shalt not make unto thee any carved image, or any likeness of anything that is in heaven above, or that is in the earth beneath, or that is in the water under the earth; thou shalt not bow down thyself to them, nor serve them; for I, the Lord thy God, am a jealous God, visiting the iniquity of the fathers upon the children unto the third and fourth generation of them that hate me; and showing mercy unto thousands of them that love me, and keep my commandments" (vv. 3-6). The primary issue in the beginning of the Ten Commandments is that no god is to be substituted for the true God. That is God's basic concern in His dealing with man.

The Bible explicitly says that no other gods exist (Deut. 6:4; Isa. 43:11; 44:6; 45:5-6). And it denounces all idols whether they are idols of stone, wood, or metal, or idols of the mind or emotions. Whether they are tangible or intangible, external or internal, all idols are prohibited in the statement: "Thou shalt have no other gods before me. Thou shalt not make unto thee any carved image."

d) Examined

A brief survey of what Scripture teaches about idolatry will help us understand what Hananiah, Azariah, and Mishael faced (the three Hebrews who were given the Babylonian names of Shadrach, Meshach, and Abednego). They knew they couldn't please God by worshiping the image of gold erected in chapter 3. Even though they didn't have God's entire revelation as we do today, they knew enough to know God's perspective on idolatry.

(1) Manifestations of idolatry

(a) Bowing down to images (Ex. 20:5)

(b) Worshiping images (Ps. 106:19-20; Isa. 44:17)

(c) Sacrificing to other gods and images (Ex. 22:20; Ps. 106:38)

(d) Worshiping other gods (Deut. 30:17)

(e) Swearing by other gods (Josh. 23:7)

(f) Walking after other gods (Deut. 8:19)

(g) Speaking in the name of other gods (Deut. 18:20)

(h) Looking to other gods (Hos. 3:1)

(i) Serving other gods (Jer. 5:19)

(j) Fearing other gods (2 Kings 17:35)

(k) Worshiping angels (Col. 2:18)

(l) Worshiping the host of heaven (Deut. 4:19)

(*m*) Worshiping devils (Matt. 4:9-10)

(*n*) Worshiping dead men (Ps. 106:28)

(*o*) Setting up idols in the heart (Ezek. 14:3-4)

(*p*) Coveting (Eph. 5:5)

(*q*) Acting like a glutton (Phil. 3:19)

(2) Condemnations of idolatry

It is condemned as:

(*a*) An abomination to God (Deut. 7:25)

(*b*) Hateful to God (Deut. 16:22)

(*c*) Vain and foolish (Ps. 115:4-8)

(*d*) Bloody (Ezek. 23:39)

(*e*) Abominable (1 Pet. 4:3)

(*f*) Unprofitable (Judg. 10:14)

(*g*) Irrational (Rom. 1:21-23)

(*h*) Defiling (Ezek. 20:7)

(3) Consequences of idolatry

(*a*) Forgetting God (Jer. 18:15)

(*b*) Going astray from God (Ezek. 44:10)

(*c*) Polluting the name of God (Ezek. 20:39)

(*d*) Defiling the sanctuary of God (Ezek. 5:11)

(*e*) Estranging oneself from God (Ezek. 14:5)

(*f*) Forsaking God (2 Kings 22:17)

(*g*) Hating God (2 Chron. 19:2-3)

(*h*) Provoking God (Deut. 31:20)

(4) Judgments on idolatry

The Bible says that idolatry will be punished.

(*a*) Judicial death (Deut. 17:2-5)

(*b*) Dreadful judgment that ends in death (Jer. 8:2)

(*c*) Banishment (Amos 5:26-27)

(*d*) Exclusion from heaven (1 Cor. 6:9-10)

(*e*) Eternal torment (Rev. 21:8)

Committing idolatry is a serious offense. The Bible warns, "Flee from idolatry" (1 Cor. 10:14), have no "fellowship with demons" (1 Cor. 10:20), and "keep yourselves from idols" (1 John 5:21). Those three commands basically mean the same thing. Idolatry is a serious matter with God.

2. Idolatry in society

Some people argue that we don't have any idols today. We live in a sophisticated society that has been predominately influenced by Christian values and truths. Still our society is filled with idols of a more subtle kind. Idolatry is external in many societies, but in others it is internal. Millions of people who would never think of bowing before a stone idol spend their lives worshiping some useless god established in their own minds.

An idol is whatever becomes more important than God. It can be a car, a hobby, a house, a spouse, or a bankbook. Let's survey some twentieth-century idols.

a) Possessions

Possessions can usurp the place of God. Do you spend more time thinking about possessions than God? Do you spend more energy on acquiring possessions than on knowing God? If so, that is a good indication you have a problem in that area.

b) Plenty

Colossians 3:5 says that covetousness is idolatry. When you covet something, you worship it, like the rich man who decided to build bigger barns to store his crops in. He planned to have so much that he could relax and eat, drink, and be merry. But the Lord replied, "Thou fool, this night thy soul will be required of thee" (Luke 12:16-21).

c) Pride

I believe the primary god of our society is the love of self. In fact, we could even say that some in our society see themselves as gods.

d) People

Some people idolize a child, a mate, a lover, or a friend. In contrast, Hannah prayed for God to give her a son for a long time and when God answered her prayer, she didn't worship the child. Rather, she gave him to the Lord's service (1 Sam. 1:9-28). Another example of one who put God before the love of his own child is Abraham. He waited for a son until he was one hundred years old. When God tested Abraham's faith by directing him to sacrifice his son, Abraham basically said, "God, I love my son, but I don't worship him. I will obey You" (Gen. 22:1-14).

That doesn't mean you shouldn't love people or be committed to them. However, you must have your priorities in the right order. Charles H. Spurgeon, the nineteenth-century English preacher, arrived with his fiancée where he was going to preach. They were separated in the jostling crowd of thousands pushing in to hear him preach. When he failed to find her after the meeting, he went to her house, where he found her pouting. Mrs. Spurgeon herself wrote, "Quietly he let me tell him how indignant I had felt. . . . [He assured] me of his deep affection for me, but [pointed] out that, before all things, he was God's servant, and I must be prepared to yield my claims to his. I never forgot the teaching of that day; I had learned my hard lesson by heart, for I do not recollect ever again seeking to assert my right to his time and attention when any service for God demanded them" (C. H. Spurgeon Autobiography, vol. 1 [Carlisle, Penn.: Banner of Truth, 1962], pp. 288-89).

e) Pleasure

Our society also worships the god of entertainment. Every time I go to an amusement park, I see people trying to escape the reality of life by living in a fantasy world. They pay a lot of money for a few moments of excitement. Unfortunately, that is how many people live. Our society is full of lovers of pleasure rather than lovers of God.

f) Projects

Some people immerse themselves in projects and organizations, such as the Parent-Teacher Association, Little League, world peace, politics, hobbies, religious programs, and the Rotary Club. Seeking for meaning, they fill their lives with projects.

g) Prominence

Other people live to be included in *Who's Who.* They want to sit at the head table at banquets and be in the social register. They love to see their names in newspapers and be chairmen of organizations.

All those gods end up trashed in an empty, burned-out life. But people will always find something to worship. The story is told about an idol-burning ceremony in the back of a church. Each person deposited his dearest possession, ambition, or achievement in a pile. People placed prized locks of hair, newly acquired Ph.D.s, favorite antiques, and coveted mink coats in a heap. Although no one could find a match, all agreed that failing to burn them didn't mean they weren't willing to give them up. Reluctantly the group drifted back to their homes. One woman didn't sleep well that night and at last convinced herself that what she had given up was not an idol at all. Early the next morning she sneaked back to the church, hoping not to be seen. When she arrived, she saw that her idol was the only one left. How stubbornly we cling to our idols!

B. Worshiping the Right God in the Wrong Way

1. Explained

The golden calf in Exodus 32 was meant to represent the true God. When Aaron and the Israelites made the golden calf, they were worshiping the right God in a wrong way. God told Saul to destroy the Amalekites but not to take any spoil. But Saul spared the king, some sheep, and some other animals. Samuel confronted Saul about his disobedience. Even though Saul claimed to have taken the animals to sacrifice to God, Samuel said, "The Lord hath torn the kingdom of Israel from thee" (1 Sam. 15:1-31). God wants us to worship Him the way He instructs us, not the way we choose.

2. Illustrated

a) In the history of the church

The medieval church worshiped symbols that were intended to represent God. The iconoclastic (Gk., *eikōn*, "image") controversy resulted from the excessive use of statues in the eighth and ninth centuries. Today, crucifixes and images of various saints constitute a kind of idolatry. Some may claim that they don't actually worship the icons, which are intended to serve as reminders. But the transition between worshiping the God behind the statue and the statue itself is subtle.

b) In the history of Israel

(1) The provision of salvation

You may remember that the Lord sent fiery serpents among the Israelites because of their rebellion against Him and Moses. Many were bitten and died. Numbers 21:7-8 says, "Therefore the people came to Moses, and said, We have sinned; for we have spoken against the Lord, and against thee; pray unto the Lord, that he take away the serpents from us. And Moses prayed for the people. And the Lord said unto Moses, Make thee a fiery serpent, and set it on a pole; and it shall come to pass, that everyone that is bitten, when he looketh upon it, shall live." The serpent was only a symbol of God's power. The power was with God. Looking at the pole demonstrated their faith.

(2) The perversion of the serpent

Later in the history of Israel, Hezekiah, king of Judah, ushered in a great revival. Second Kings 18:4 says, "He removed the high places, and broke the images, and cut down the idols, and broke in pieces the bronze serpent that Moses had made; for unto those days the children of Israel did burn incense to it: and he called it Nehushtan" ("the little brass thing"). What began as a symbol became an idol. That is always the danger of an icon.

Both worshiping a false god and worshiping the true God in a wrong way are forbidden in Scripture. We'll look at how Daniel's three friends faced the issue of idolatry. They were well educated in Hebrew doctrine and knew exactly how God regarded idols.

Lesson

I. THE CEREMONY (vv. 1-3)

A. The Act of Idolatry (v. 1)

"Nebuchadnezzar, the king, made an image of gold, whose height was threescore cubits, and the breadth of it six cubits; he set it up in the plain of Dura, in the province of Babylon."

Nebuchadnezzar was the king of the Babylonian Empire, which included much of the Middle East. That powerful monarch had a huge image of himself made. That idolatrous act seems inconsistent with his confession to Daniel in the previous chapter. In chapter 2 Daniel tells Nebuchadnezzar the dream about an image made of gold, brass, silver, iron, and clay. He explained that the different sections of the image represented four world empires that would arise in turn and ultimately be destroyed by a stone cut without hands. Because Nebuchadnezzar knew Daniel was telling him what his own seers and magicians did not understand, he "fell upon his face, and worshiped Daniel . . . and said, Of a truth it is that your God is the God of gods, and the Lord of kings, and a revealer of secrets, seeing thou couldest reveal this secret" (2:46-47). But two verses later he builds an idol to himself. Even a demonstration of the power of God couldn't subdue his ego. In fact, when Daniel told him that he represented the head of gold (vv. 36-38), Nebuchadnezzar probably thought, *I'm the head —everyone else is inferior to me*. Therefore he built an entire image of gold.

1. The image

a) Its dimensions

"[The] height was threescore cubits, and the breadth of it six cubits" (v. 1).

The image was probably a huge human form. A cubit was measured from the elbow to the end of the hand, approximately eighteen inches. So sixty cubits would equal ninety feet, much taller than a sixty-foot telephone pole. Because the image was only six cubits wide (nine feet), it was a tall, thin statue. Its ten-to-one proportions are quite different from the five-to-one proportions of most human beings. It is possible that such a great height indicates that the statue stood upon a high pedestal.

b) Its construction

"An image of gold" (v. 1).

I don't believe that the image was solid gold, because that would have been prohibitive in terms of cost, as well as construction and transportation. In ancient times images of wood were commonly overlaid with gold. Isaiah 40:19 and 41:7 speak of wooden idols overlaid with gold. Even the cost of overlaid gold would have been incredible. The cost and difficulty of mining gold in ancient times made the metal extremely valuable.

The Significance of the Sexagesimal System

The dimensions of sixty cubits and six cubits illustrate the Babylonian sexagesimal system of numerics (see p. 22). Our decimal system is based on tens, but they had a system based on sixes. That evidence supports the authenticity of Daniel as truly representative of Babylonian times. Higher critics date the writing of Daniel close to the time of Christ so that they can claim it is an after-the-fact historical account rather than divine prophecy. However, the text itself doesn't warrant that. (For more information on the dating of Daniel, see Josh McDowell's *Daniel in the Critic's Den* [San Bernardino, Calif.: Here's Life, 1979].)

c) Its location

"He set it up in the plain of Dura, in the province of Babylon" (v. 1).

The plain of Dura was located near the city of Babylon. Since Nebuchadnezzar's statue was made out of gold, those who conquered Babylon plundered it.

The plain of Dura was quite flat. Surely such a statue would have been visible for a great distance. Imagine how the bright sun in that region made its gold sparkle in an incredible display of grandeur.

2. The intentions

What was Nebuchadnezzar trying to accomplish with this huge image? I believe he had some reasons for having it made. He was an intelligent man—one of the world's greatest architects, statesmen, and military strategists.

a) Unifying the nation

A leader unifies his nation around a common objective, and Nebuchadnezzar wanted his subjects to bow down to him. In a similar manner, the Caesars used emperor worship to unify the entire Roman Empire.

b) Verifying loyalty

Nebuchadnezzar wanted all his leaders to bow down to him to test their loyalty and faithfulness to him.

c) Preventing factions

Nebuchadnezzar wanted a single religion because a division over religion could fracture his empire.

d) Glorifying self

Nebuchadnezzar had an incredible ego. Having seen himself as the head of gold, he decided to make an image so that everyone could worship him. He was like Herod in Acts 12. After he delivered a speech in all his majesty, the people said, "The voice of a god, and not of a man" (v. 22). He readily accepted that praise. The result of his pride is recorded in verse 23:

"Immediately an angel of the Lord smote him, because he gave not God the glory, and he was eaten of worms, and died." Although Nebuchadnezzar wasn't eaten by worms, he did experience divine punishment in Daniel 4.

The conflict in chapter 3 is between worshiping the true God and worshiping this self-centered king. This is a choice everyone makes—either worshiping the true God or false gods. Even Christians can be lured to worship false gods.

B. The Acceptance of the Invitation (vv. 2-3)

1. The recipients (v. 2)

"Nebuchadnezzar, the king, sent to gather together."

a) "The princes"

The princes were the top governors of the provinces in the Babylonian Empire.

b) "The governors, and the captains"

As best we can determine, the governors and captains were secondary rulers in subdivisions of the provinces.

c) "The judges"

The judges were the chief arbitrators or provincial counselors throughout the empire.

d) "The treasurers"

The treasurers were the masters of the government funds.

e) "The counselors"

The counselors were the lawyers who made up the cabinets and the senates.

f) "The sheriffs"

The sheriffs were the officers who carried out the judicial sentences.

Daniel 3:2 concludes by saying that he invited "all the rulers of the provinces, to come to the dedication of the image which Nebuchadnezzar, the king, had set up." Wanting to secure everyone's allegiance, Nebuchadnezzar invited all his leadership to the ceremony.

2. The subtle repetition (v. 3)

"The princes, the governors, and captains, the judges, the treasurers, the counselors, the sheriffs, and all the rulers of the provinces were gathered together unto the dedication of the image that Nebuchadnezzar, the king, had set up; and they stood before the image that Nebuchadnezzar had set up."

Why does the passage repeat the previous information? When the Septuagint (the Greek version of the Old Testament) was written, the translators left out verse 3 because they believed it was unnecessary to repeat the listing in verse 2 to verse 3. But the repetition of verse 3 is an almost humorous insight into the lack of personal integrity among the leaders of the empire. It indicates that although they were all respected people, none had the courage to say no. They all came, spinelessly following the leadership of Nebuchadnezzar. Only three men in the entire Babylonian empire had the integrity to say no.

Focusing on the Facts

1. What do all races or ethnic groups have in common (see p. 66)?
2. If people refuse to worship the true God, what will they worship (see pp. 66-67)?
3. Explain the cycle of idolatry. Why does man create a god like himself (see p. 67)?
4. What is the ultimate form of rebellion (see p. 67)?

5. The first two of the Ten Commandments indicate what basic concern of God (see p. 68)?
6. What did Daniel and his three friends know about idolatry? How were they aware of that (see pp. 69-71)?
7. How is idolatry judged (see p. 71)?
8. What are some twentieth-century idols (see pp. 71-73)?
9. Give a biblical example of someone who set his love for God before his love for his child (see p. 72).
10. Besides worshiping wrong gods, what is another form of idolatry? Explain how Saul was guilty (see p. 74; 1 Sam. 15:1-31).
11. According to 2 Kings 18:4, what object did the Israelites worship (see p. 75)?
12. How is Nebuchadnezzar's statue inconsistent with his discussion with Daniel in chapter 2 (see p. 76)?
13. Describe Nebuchadnezzar's image (see pp. 76-78).
14. What is significant about the use of a sexagesimal numeric system in the book of Daniel (see p. 77)?
15. What was Nebuchadnezzar trying to accomplish by erecting the image (see pp. 78-79)?
16. Explain the significance of the repetition of the Babylonian rulers listed in Daniel 3:2-3 (see p. 80).

Pondering the Principles

1. Examine the list of twentieth-century gods on pages 71-73. What things do you idolize? Do you spend more time caring for them than your relationship with God? If they distract you from prayer and the Word, are you willing to part with them? If you value them above communion with God, why is that so? What can you do today to rearrange your priorities? Decide how to motivate yourself to maintain them. Establish goals with specific objectives to assist you in meeting them, and find someone who will hold you accountable to your commitment.

2. How would others evaluate your integrity? Do you know why you believe what you do? Are you willing to stand for what you believe, or do you bend under pressure? Imagine yourself with a group of non-Christians at work or in your neighborhood. If they ridiculed you for standing for Christ, how would you defend your faith? Read 1 Peter 3:14-15 and write out a few sentences that could serve as an effective defense in situations of intimidation, ridicule, and honest questions.

5
Uncompromising Faith in the Fiery Furnace—Part 2

Outline

Introduction

Review
I. The Ceremony (vv. 1-3)

Lesson
II. The Command (vv. 4-5)
   A. The Call of the Herald (v. 4)
   B. The Cue by the Orchestra (v. 5)
   C. The Consequences of Disobedience (v. 6)
   D. The Conformity of the People (v. 7)
III. The Conspiracy (vv. 8-12)
   A. The Context of the Accusation (v. 8)
   B. The Cause of the Accusation (vv. 9-12*a*)
   C. The Content of the Accusation (v. 12*b*)
      1. Their lack of regard
      2. Their limit of religion
IV. The Coercion (vv. 13-15)
   A. The Report Confirmed (vv. 13-14)
   B. The Response Commanded (v. 15)
V. The Courage (vv. 16-18)
   A. Admitting Their Fault (v. 16)
   B. Affirming Their Faith (vv. 17-18)
      1. The expression of commitment
      2. The examples of commitment
         a) Job
         b) Paul
         c) Martin Luther

Introduction

Our decisions, attitudes, and behavior are determined by one of two things: external pressure or internal principles. The battle between those two conflicting elements occurs all the time. Since we are often skilled at self-justification, it is easy for us to succumb to external pressure, which we try to redefine as internal principle. We need to determine the principles by which we live. Do we do what we do and say what we say because we have a specific conviction or because we feel pressure from the outside?

If you are in a business situation and have the opportunity to profit by compromising, do you succumb to that external pressure or do you act on what you know to be the proper internal principle? This is a key issue for Christians. If the world ever needed people who operate on an internal principle, it needs them now. We all become weary of people who succumb to external pressures and rarely do what they have promised or what they say they believe.

As we examine the third chapter of Daniel, we will study three young men who functioned on internal principles and ignored external pressure. As followers of Jesus Christ, we have a lot to learn from these three men. I want you to see yourself in the context of this passage. I'm not so concerned that you see Shadrach, Meshach, and Abednego as much as you evaluate how you would respond in a similar situation. It doesn't matter what these three young Hebrew men did unless we can learn something from their example to help us in the way we confront our world. Do we put God first? Do we put His Word first? Do we act on internal principles, or do we compromise as a result of external pressure?

The story of the fiery furnace has eight key features: the ceremony, the command, the conspiracy, the coercion, the courage, the consequences, the companion, and the commendation.

Review

I. THE CEREMONY (vv. 1-3; see pp. 76-80)

Lesson

II. THE COMMAND (vv. 4-5)

A. The Call of the Herald (v. 4)

"Then an herald cried aloud, To you it is commanded, O people, nations, and languages."

"Peoples, nations, and languages" is a common form of address used in speaking to an assembly of people. It is also used in verses 7 and 29, as well as in 4:1 and 6:25. The herald called together this group of people to give them a command.

B. The Cue by the Orchestra (v. 5)

"That at that time that ye hear the sound of the horn, pipe, lyre, sackbut, psaltery, dulcimer, and all kinds of music, ye fall down and worship the golden image that Nebuchadnezzar, the king, hath set up."

Desiring the people's submission at a precise moment, Nebuchadnezzar instructed his royal orchestra to give the cue. This orchestra, however, would have had a much different sound than what we are accustomed to, because at that particular time in history, the harmonic relationship between musical tones was not understood. For this reason, the music would not have had the sweet harmonies we know; it would have sounded quite dissonant. The music was designed to draw everyone's attention to the image they were to bow before.

The orchestra consisted of the following instruments: a "horn," which had a relatively low sound, and a "pipe," which was a flute with a higher sound. The "lyre" was a small harp producing high sounds. The "sackbut" is best understood to refer to an ancient triangular harp. The "psaltery" was a harp with a sounding board that produced a lower sound than a lyre. The "dulcimer" was basically a bagpipe. At the time all these instruments sounded, everyone was instantly to fall down and worship the image.

C. The Consequences of Disobedience (v. 6)

"Whoever falleth not down and worshipeth, shall the same hour be cast into the midst of a burning fiery furnace."

I don't know what else a fiery furnace could do except burn, so I assume that the word *burning* is used to intensify the consequence. Refusing to bow down would constitute a treasonous act and the offender would be thrown into the fiery furnace. Standing in opposition to the authority of Nebuchadnezzar would result in death.

D. The Conformity of the People (v. 7)

"Therefore, at that time when all the people heard the sound of the horn, pipe, lyre, sackbut, psaltery, and all kinds of music, all the people, the nations, and the languages fell down and worshiped the golden image that Nebuchadnezzar, the king, had set up."

Unfortunately, most people respond to the pressure of external circumstances. They conform to whatever is required of them, rather than to some internal principle. We meet in this verse a group of intimidated people whose typical approach to life was to do whatever was expedient. Men often compromise internal principles because of external pressure. They willingly bow to the system of authority, because they fear the loss of their position.

However, some did not compromise. Everyone fell down except three Jewish men.

III. THE CONSPIRACY (vv. 8-12)

A. The Context of the Accusation (v. 8)

"Wherefore, at that time certain Chaldeans came near, and accused the Jews."

Probably as many as seventy-five young men were taken captive from Judah to Babylon to be trained to work in Jewish affairs. But out of all of them, only four, Daniel and his three friends, are recorded as having been uncompromising. We assume that the rest of the Jewish captives bowed down with everyone else. They evidently chose to compromise their principles in their desire to be promoted within the system. Three young Jewish men stood their ground. (Daniel apparently was not present.) They demonstrated tremendous conviction for young men only about twenty years of age.

Notice that those who made the accusation were Chaldeans, who were influential in Babylonian culture. However, when these three young men exhibited great character along with Daniel, they were elevated to high places, possibly even above the Chaldeans. Daniel 2:49 records that promotion: "Then Daniel requested of the king, and he set Shadrach, Meshach, and Abednego over the affairs of the province of Babylon; but Daniel sat in the gate of the king." Daniel was promoted to prime minister of Babylon, and the other three were placed in leadership over the province of Babylon. The Chaldeans resented that and accused the three. They spoke to the king as if they were defending him, appearing to aid their king in enforcing obedience to his command.

B. The Cause of the Accusation (vv. 9-12a)

"They spoke and said to the king, Nebuchadnezzar, O king, live forever. Thou, O king, hast made a decree, that every man that shall hear the sound of the horn, pipe, lyre, sackbut, psaltery, and dulcimer, and all kinds of music, shall fall down and worship the golden image; and whoever falleth not down and worshipeth, that he should be cast into the midst of a burning fiery furnace. There are certain Jews whom thou hast set over the affairs of the province of Babylon, Shadrach, Meshach, and Abed-nego."

After the Chaldeans reiterated the standard the king had set, they revealed the issue that bothered them: they were envious that Jewish captives would be given high-ranking positions. They despised having imported hostages rule over them. Falling prey to the sin of jealousy, they brought their complaint before the king.

C. The Content of the Accusation (v. 12b)

1. Their lack of regard

"These men, O king, have not regarded thee."

The first part of the threefold accusation was that Shadrach, Meshach, and Abednego refused to show respect due the king. But that was not true. They had demonstrated the same type of submission taught by our Lord in Matthew 22:21: "Render, therefore, unto Caesar the things which are Caesar's; and unto God, the things that are God's." They had unquestionably fulfilled their responsibility to the king insofar as it didn't violate their responsibility to God. They were good citizens. They had responded to the king appropriately by attending his ceremony.

The rest of the Chaldean's accusation was true, however.

2. Their limit of religion

"They serve not thy gods, nor worship the golden image which thou hast set up."

These three young men knew the price of disobedience and were willing to pay it. They regarded their principles so highly that they remained standing while the entire mass of people bowed down. They were prepared to face a fiery furnace. That's the kind of character that lives by internal principles, not external pressure. Consider the situation: Nebuchadnezzar was their friend and benefactor and their destiny was in his hands. Resisting Nebuchadnezzar would be useless; they had no other resource for protection. Furthermore, future advancement in their careers in Babylon was dependent on their allegiance. They could have said to themselves, *An idol isn't anything anyway, so why should we worry about it? We'll just kneel down with everyone else, except we'll pray to the true God. If we don't bow down, we're going to play into the hands of these jealous Chaldeans.* Many things may have pressured them, yet they were resolute and uncompromising.

You may have wondered why Nebuchadnezzar was disturbed by three people who disobeyed. But an egomaniac can't stand even one person who doesn't conform, let alone three. Nebuchadnezzar would not stand for anything except absolute submission from everyone.

IV. THE COERCION (vv. 13-15)

A. The Report Confirmed (vv. 13-14)

Enraged at the report of the Chaldeans, Nebuchadnezzar summoned the three who had been accused: "Then Nebuchadnezzar in his rage and fury commanded to bring Shadrach, Meshach, and Abed-nego. Then they brought these men before the king. Nebuchadnezzar spoke and said unto them, Is it true, O Shadrach, Meshach, and Abed-nego, do not yet serve my gods, nor worship the golden image which I have set up?" Notice that he dropped the first accusation the Chaldeans made about the Jewish men not regarding the king. He knew that wasn't true.

B. The Response Commanded (v. 15)

Deciding to give them a second chance, the king repeats his command: "Now, if ye be ready that at that time that ye heard the sound of the horn, pipe, lyre, sackbut, psaltery, and dulcimer, and all kinds of music, to fall down and worship the image which I have made, well; but if ye worship not, ye shall be cast the same hour into the midst of a burning fiery furnace. And who is that God, that shall deliver you out of my hands?" Nebuchadnezzer had a short memory. He forgot that they worshiped the same God who was able to reveal his dreams and visions. To his credit Nebuchadnezzar did seem to be somewhat of a just man by his desire to know if the accusation was true. At least he gave them a chance to speak for themselves before he threw them into the fiery furnace.

Blinded by his fury, the proud king actually pitted his power against the power of God. Once he had pitted himself against the eternal God, he had met his match. Had he forgotten that Daniel's God was greater than all the gods of Babylon?

V. THE COURAGE (vv. 16-18)

A. Admitting Their Fault (v. 16)

"Shadrach, Meshach, and Abed-nego answered and said to the king, O Nebuchadnezzar, we are not careful to answer thee in this matter."

Their answer wasn't arrogant; they simply stated that they had nothing to say. They admitted their guilt. They had faithfully served Nebuchadnezzar as far as they could. But serving his gods and worshiping his idols was beyond their allegiance.

B. Affirming Their Faith (vv. 17-18)

"If it be so, our God, whom we serve, is able to deliver us from the burning fiery furnace, and he will deliver us out of thine hand, O king. But if not, be it known unto thee, O king, that we will not serve thy gods, nor worship the golden image which thou hast set up."

1. The expression of commitment

With an air of finality, the three youths made no rationalization or compromise. They offered no defense, only the statement that the God whom they served was greater than Nebuchadnezzar. What faith and courage these young men had! We can easily agree with what they said in the comfortable society we live in, but these men faced a stiff penalty for their testimony. Their faith held firm in the worst moment because they were committed to their internal principles. They had been taught the Word of God and therefore knew how to respond. They would not compromise no matter what the external pressures were. Their conviction was not dependent on whether they were delivered by a miracle. They would accept God's will even if it meant death.

2. The examples of commitment

If we can give this world anything, it's an uncompromising spirit of integrity. However, we often bow to twentieth-century idols to receive what we desire. Shadrach, Meshach, and Abednego knew that the heathen king was spiritually blind and that their lengthy explanations were useless. They simply committed themselves to God in much the same way as did these godly men.

a) Job

The three Jewish men reflected the trust of Job, who declared in Job 13:15, "Though he slay me, yet will I trust him." They knew that obeying the truth of God was more important than being concerned about what might happen to them. We should strive to develop uncompromising lives that will not bow to any idol, no matter what the cost. No compromise is needed for one who understands that God is just as good when He doesn't heal as when He does, is just as loving when He doesn't provide what we desire as when He does, and is just as gracious when He says no as when He says yes.

b) Paul

In Philippians 1:21 Paul says, "For to me to live is Christ, and to die is gain." The fear of death never forced Paul to compromise. He laid his head on a block and an ax severed it from his body—he never compromised. Is our faith so real that no price can make us bow down?

c) Martin Luther

Luther, in his loneliness as he faced the inevitable hour of excommunication at the Diet of Worms, wrote to the Elector Fredrick, "You ask me what I shall do if I am called by the emperor. I will go down if I am too sick to stand on my feet. If Caesar calls me, God calls me. If violence is used, as well it may be, I commend my cause to God. He lives and reigns who saved the three youths from the fiery furnace of the king of Babylon, and if He will not save me, my head is worth nothing compared with Christ. This is no time to think of safety. I must take care that the gospel is not brought into contempt by our fear to confess and seal our teaching with our blood" (Roland H. Bainton, *Here I Stand: A Life of Martin Luther* [New York: Abingdon, 1950], p. 174). Martin Luther took his cue from those three Jewish men. He didn't say, "Deliver me"; he said, "If God wants to take my life, it is a small thing."

Like those great men of God, we're to resist the pressure of the world to bow to its idols. Someone once wrote, "The dearest idol I have known, what e'er that idol be, help me to tear it from its throne and worship only Thee." No wonder John closes his marvelous epistle with the command "keep yourselves from idols" (1 John 5:21).

92

VI. THE CONSEQUENCES (vv. 19-23)

A. The Fury of the King (vv. 19-20)

1. His countenance (v. 19*a*)

"Then was Nebuchadnezzar full of fury, and the form of his visage was changed against Shadrach, Meshach, and Abed-nego."

In verse 13 Nebuchadnezzar had rage and fury, but now he was full of anger. For this reason, his visage was changed, which means that he was so angry his face became distorted. Having been thwarted in his effort to have everyone worship him, he expressed intense rage.

2. His commands (vv. 19*b*-20)

a) To turn up the heat (v. 19*b*)

"Therefore, he spoke, and commanded that they should heat the furnace seven times more than it was usually heated."

Though it may appear logical, Nebuchadnezzar's reaction was actually an irrational extension of his anger. If he had wanted to torture them, he should have turned the heat down. Heating the furnace seven times hotter would only result in instant death. In a court full of spineless flatterers and men pleasers stood these three young men. Their refusal to submit to Nebuchadnezzar's immoral request caused him to lose rational control.

b) To execute the youths (v. 20)

"He commanded the most mighty men that were in his army to bind Shadrach, Meshach, and Abed-nego, and to cast them into the burning fiery furnace."

The furnace was probably a pit that had an opening below where the fire was stoked, and an opening at the top served as an air draft. Nebuchadnezzar could have stood on a balcony and watched what was happening through the top opening. The strong men who were commanded to tie up the three Jewish men and then cast them into the furnace were probably the king's best soldiers—perhaps his personal bodyguards.

B. The Faith of the Youths (v. 21)

"Then these men were bound in their coats, their stockings, and their turbans, and their other garments, and were cast into the midst of the burning fiery furnace."

The fact that the three young men were still in their coats, stockings, and turbans indicates they had specially dressed for the occasion. Their willingness to dress appropriately for the king's ceremony tells us they responded to the king. They were not rebellious; they just couldn't bow down to the image because that would constitute disobedience to God. The king was so furious that he didn't bother to have them change clothes for their execution. They were hastily bound and thrown into the fiery furnace.

The three young men probably concluded that God was not going to save them *from* the fire, but no doubt they hoped to be saved *in* the fire. That's precisely what happened. Knowing they were not going to escape the experience, they faithfully resigned themselves to suffer for God's glory. Perhaps they remembered the comforting words of Isaiah 43:2, "When thou walkest through the fire, thou shalt not be burned, neither shall the flame kindle upon thee."

C. The Failure of the Soldiers (vv. 22-23)

"Therefore, because the king's commandment was urgent and the furnace exceedingly hot, the flame of the fire slew those men that took up Shadrach, Meshach, and Abed-nego. And these three men, Shadrach, Meshach, and Abed-nego, fell down bound into the midst of the burning fiery furnace."

The soldiers that threw them in all burned to death because of the intense heat. However, the three youths on the inside did not burn.

VII. THE COMPANION (vv. 24-25)

"Nebuchadnezzar, the king, was astounded, and rose up in haste, and spoke, and said unto his counselors, Did not we cast three men, bound, into the midst of the fire? They answered and said unto the king, True, O king. He answered and said, Lo, I see four men loose, walking in the midst of the fire, and they have no hurt; and the form of the fourth is like a son of the gods."

Although Nebuchadnezzar was upset when this confrontation began, he became startled at this point. He was astonished by the presence of a fourth individual in the fire. Rather than being bound and lying down, the three Jewish men were loose and walking around. They appeared to be patiently waiting and enjoying each other's company. The fourth man in the fire had the appearance of a god. But who was he?

A. His Identity Discussed

Nebuchadnezzar was a pagan. He did not know the Son of God. He wouldn't have understood an Old Testament appearance of Christ, such as in Genesis 18. I believe Nebuchadnezzar concluded that he had seen an angelic being, because in verse 28 of this same chapter he used the word *angel*. Nebuchadnezzar believed the fourth person was a supernatural messenger of God. Some believe he was Christ; others believe he was an angel.

B. His Intent Determined

I believe God sent an angel into that fiery furnace to explain to those three young men what was going on: "I'm sent from God to preserve you in the midst of this fire. You're not going to be burned." Sending an angel wasn't anything new. For example, Elijah had been similarly honored by having God's angels personally serve him food at a time when he was terribly discouraged (1 Kings 19:4-7).

Hebrews 13:5 quotes the Lord as having said, "I will never leave thee, nor forsake thee." God chooses to send His angels to care for us in the midst of dire circumstances. How wonderful to know that we go through every experience with God! The hotter the fire becomes, the sweeter the fellowship. I can testify that whenever I have taken a stand for something unpopular yet biblical, I have a tremendous sense of divine companionship and the strengthening of God. This is what Peter had in mind when he spoke of "the Spirit of glory and of God" resting upon those who are persecuted for the name of Christ (1 Pet. 4:14).

VIII. THE COMMENDATION (vv. 26-30)

A. The Investigation by the Rulers (vv. 26-27)

"Then Nebuchadnezzar came near to the mouth of the burning fiery furnace, and spoke, and said, Shadrach, Meshach, and Abed-nego, ye servants of the Most High God, come forth, and come here. Then Shadrach, Meshach, and Abed-nego came forth from the midst of the fire. And the princes, governors, and captains, and the king's counselors, being gathered together, saw these men, upon whose bodies the fire had no power, nor was an hair of their head singed, neither were their coats changed, nor the smell of fire had passed on them."

When I was in college, I bought a coat on sale at a store that had partially burned down. I wore that coat for about three years, but it never stopped smelling of smoke. If you've ever had a fire in your home you know it is virtually impossible to remove the smell of smoke from clothes. It was truly a miracle for all to see that the three young men had escaped without their hair being singed or their garments burned.

B. The Exaltation by Nebuchadnezzar (vv. 28-30)

1. His reasons (v. 28)

a) The sovereignty of God (v. 28a)

"Then Nebuchadnezzar spoke, and said, Blessed be the God of Shadrach, Meshach, and Abed-nego, who hath sent his angel and delivered his servants."

Although he called their God "the Most High God" (v. 26), Nebuchadnezzar was not abandoning his polytheism; he merely put God on top of the pile of other gods he worshiped. He was not acknowledging that the Lord is the one true God (apparently that came later in Daniel 4), but only that He was the supreme deity. The king retained his traditional worship of many gods. He was acknowledging what theologians call "henotheism," which basically is the belief that certain peoples or nations have their own gods. Making room for the God of Shadrach, Meshach, and Abed-nego, Nebuchadnezzar was willing to accept the God of Israel as the Most High God of all the gods. However, that is far from saying He's the only God.

b) The submissiveness of His servants (v. 28b)

"His servants who trusted in him, and hath changed the king's word, and yielded their bodies, that they might not serve nor worship any god, except their own God."

The statement "yielded their bodies" sounds like Romans 12:1-2: "Present your bodies a living sacrifice. . . . And be not conformed to this world." That is exactly what they did. Impressed with such commitment, Nebuchadnezzar blessed their God. We, too, can make an impact on the pagan world by living an uncompromising life. Even in their unbelief, the unsaved will have to say that our God is the Most High God.

2. His decree (vv. 29-30)

"Therefore, I make a decree, that every people, nation, and language, who speak anything amiss against the God of Shadrach, Meshach, and Abed-nego, shall be cut in pieces, and their houses shall be made a refuse heap, because there is no other god that can deliver after this sort. Then the king promoted Shadrach, Meshach, and Abed-nego in the province of Babylon."

Because the three Jewish men were already rulers, their promotion must have been something special. If you believe the Chaldeans were unhappy at the beginning of chapter 3, imagine how they felt at the end of chapter 3! The king declared that anyone who showed disrespect toward the God of the Jewish people would be cut in pieces and have their houses turned into a dung pile—the ultimate desecration. Nebuchadnezzar wasn't naive; he was determined to be nice to this God. If ever he wanted anything in the future, he figured he would need this God on his side. Such a calculating action reminds me of one of the coaches in the National Football League who, when he was asked why he always had a Christian minister on the sideline, said, "I'm not even sure if I believe in God, but in case there is one, I want Him on my side."

Conclusion

You and I will probably never face a fiery furnace. But we are going to face fiery trials (1 Pet. 4:12), which can come from several sources. First of all, Satan afflicts us. He afflicted Jesus and tempted Him. Peter said that Satan was "like a roaring lion walketh about, seeking whom he may devour" (1 Pet. 5:8). He is "the accuser of our brethren" (Rev. 12:10). He wants to plant evil thoughts (Gen. 3:1-5). He sent a messenger to act as a thorn in Paul's flesh (2 Cor. 12:7). Therefore Satan is going to afflict us through the avenue of the flesh. Second, the world is going to entice and intimidate us through pleasure and persecution, hoping to get us to compromise (1 John 2:15-16; Rev. 2:10). Third, even God will bring trials into our life, testing our faith. Hebrews 12:6-8 says that God disciplines us because we're His children.

We will all have trials. Some come from Satan, some come from the world, and some God allows. But the end result is that we may be refined, courageously standing without compromising. The hymn "How Firm A Foundation" says it well:

When through fiery trials thy pathway shall lie,
My grace, all sufficient, shall be thy supply,
The flame shall not hurt thee; I only design
Thy dross to consume, and thy gold to refine.

Focusing on the Facts

1. Our decisions, attitudes, and actions be determined by what (see p. 84)?
2. What did Nebuchadnezzar demand of all the people in Babylon (see pp. 85-86)?
3. What were to be the consequences for not obeying Nebuchadnezzar's demand (see p. 86)?
4. How did almost everyone respond? Evidently, how did the majority of Jewish captives respond? Why (see pp. 86-87)?
5. Why did the Chaldeans expose the Jewish men who had refused to bow to the image (see p. 88)?
6. What part of the accusation was not true? Why (see pp. 88-90, 94)?
7. What is impressive about the three Jewish men who knew the price of their disobedience (see p. 89)?
8. What were some of the issues that could have motivated Shadrach, Meshach, and Abednego to compromise (see p. 89)?
9. Why was Nebuchadnezzar not content to ignore the few men who acted disobediently (see p. 89)?
10. In which of Nebuchadnezzar's actions can you see a degree of justice (see p. 90)?
11. Did the three men offer any excuses? What did they admit (see p. 90)?
12. Why did the faith of the three youths hold true in the worst moment? Their conviction was not dependent upon what (see pp. 90-91)?
13. Give an example of someone who demonstrated a similar kind of uncompromising faith from the Bible or from the history of the church (see pp. 91-92).
14. What is significant about the description of the clothing that the Jewish men were wearing when they were bound (see p. 94)?
15. What happened to the soldiers who threw the men into the furnace (see pp. 94-95)?
16. What startled Nebuchadnezzar as he watched the men in the furnace (see p. 95)?

17. Who might have been the fourth person in the furnace (see p. 95)?
18. What often comes as the result of increasing persecution (1 Pet. 4:14; see p. 96)?
19. After the miraculous deliverance, what did the king and his advisors notice in their investigation of the three men (see p. 96)?
20. Explain why Nebuchadnezzar's response was not indicative of true conversion (see p. 97).
21. Why did Nebuchadnezzar bless the God of Israel (see pp. 96-98)?
22. What group of people was probably upset about the promotion that Shadrach, Meshach, and Abednego received? Why (see p. 98)?
23. What are the three sources of trials that the Christian faces? What is God's purpose in trials (see p. 98)?

Pondering the Principles

1. What directs your words and actions—internal principles, external pressure, or a combination of both? Do you put God and His Word first, or do you find yourself often compromising to maintain or upgrade your position in the world? Which is most important? Why? Think through some issues that are pressuring you—either directly or indirectly—to compromise. What will be the consequences of compromising from a human perspective and a divine perspective? What things can you put into practice to strengthen the effect of internal principles in your life? Prayerfully meditate on 2 Peter 1:3-7.

2. According to James 1:2-3 and 1 Peter 1:6-7, what is the purpose of trials? Do you readily accept their productive work in your life? Knowing that God has a positive reason for allowing them, would you be justified in complaining about them? Consider a trial that you are currently experiencing or have recently gone through. Have you acquired any spiritual insights? Are you seeking to allow God to build your character from it (Rom. 5:3-4)? In developing a proper perspective on facing trials, prayerfully meditate upon 2 Corinthians 4:8-18. Allow those powerful words to motivate you to persevere and trust in God, "who will not allow you to be tempted beyond what you are able, but with the temptation will provide the way of escape also, that you may be able to endure it" (1 Cor. 10:13, NASB).

6
Daniel in the Lions' Den

Outline

Introduction
A. The Inevitable Mortality of Governments
B. The Independent Sovereignty of God
   1. Isaiah
      a) The nations as drops and dust
      b) The nations as dying grass
   2. Daniel
      a) The reign of God in history
      b) The remains of Nebuchadnezzar from history

Lesson
I. The Promotion (vv. 1-3)
   A. The Superior Authority Over Daniel
      1. His title
      2. His territory
      3. His traits
   B. The Special Abilities of Daniel
      1. He was a fine statesman
      2. He possessed the right attitude
      3. He had previous experience
   C. The Strategic Appointment of Daniel
II. The Plot (vv. 4-9)
   A. The Conspiracy (v. 4)
   B. The Conclusion (v. 5)
   C. The Consultation (vv. 6-7)
   D. The Commitment (vv. 8-9)
III. The Perseverance (vv. 10-11)
   A. The Pattern Established
   B. The Priority Established

Introduction

A. The Inevitable Mortality of Governments

Nations rise and fall with great regularity. Consider the empires of the Hittites, the Egyptians, the Assyrians, and the Babylonians. They were followed by the empires of the Medes and the Persians, the Greeks, and then the Romans. In the Western Hemisphere, we find tales of the great Mayan, Inca, and Aztec civilizations, but little trace of them remains except for archaeological artifacts and ruins.

Some of you may have lived through the greatness of England and France. Italy was a major power that threatened to dominate Europe under the leadership of Mussolini. Germany's Hitler believed he could conquer the world with his Aryan philosophy. Indeed, nations rise and fall. Today, even America itself may be on the wane.

B. The Independent Sovereignty of God

What happens to the nations is in God's predetermined plan for history. The rise and fall of nations has little to do with the ongoing existence of the people of God. For instance, consider the fall of Babylon recorded in Daniel 5: at the height of its glory, Babylon fell to the control of the Medo-Persians. That incident had little impact on what God did with His people, because Daniel rode through the ebb and flow of those nations. As we come to chapter 6, we enter into the second of four empires represented by the breast and arms of silver that belonged to the image of Daniel 2—Medo-Persia. Still, we see Daniel serving as prime minister to the new regime, just as he did with Babylon.

Is America Indispensable to God's Plan?

Across America and around the world exists a preoccupation among many Christian peoples with the preservation of certain nations. Many attempt to equate America with the church, or America with the plan of God, but doing so isn't right. Nations come and go, and God's work goes on. No nation is significant compared to the eternal plan of God.

1. Isaiah

   a) The nations as drops and dust

   Isaiah 40 speaks of the insignificance of nations compared to the sovereignty of God: "Behold, the nations are like a drop in a bucket, and are counted as the small dust of the balance" (v. 15). Nations are like one drop that spills out of a bucket. The only word I can think of to describe the nations is inconsequential. They are like dust on a scale. When God weighs out the history of humanity, the nations are insignificant. One drop of a nation is inconsequential compared to the flood of God's redemptive plan.

b) The nations as dying grass

Furthermore, Isaiah compares the nations to grass that withers, dies, and fades away (v. 7). When you think back to Nimrod, Sennacherib, Nebuchadnezzar, Cyrus, Artaxerxes, Alexander, the Caesars, the pharaohs, Napoleon, Churchill, Mussolini, Hitler, Mao, and Khrushchev, it is amazing to see how they and their nations come and go, yet God's work still goes on.

2. Daniel

a) The reign of God in history

From Daniel 4 you may remember this great statement: "This matter is by the decree of the watchers, and the demand by the word of the holy ones, to the intent that the living may know that the Most High ruleth in the kingdom of men, and giveth it to whomsoever He will" (v. 17). God rules in history and, though nations come and go, God's redemptive plan will continue to unfold on schedule.

The people of God transcend the rise and fall of nations. That's a great hope for us. We see this illustrated in Daniel's life: Though Babylon had fallen —the head of gold crushed (cf. 2:36-38), and the times of the Gentiles had moved into phase two, Daniel was right where God wanted him. God remains unencumbered by the decisions of men.

b) The remains of Nebuchadnezzar from history

Nebuchadnezzar's many monuments provided justification for his boast, "Is not this great Babylon, that I have built?" (Dan. 4:30). Nebuchadnezzar attempted to build a lasting empire, but all that remains of his efforts are ruins.

God's people and plan transcend the historical activities of the nations. That is why Daniel survived in the midst of the Medo-Persian Empire.

Lesson

I. THE PROMOTION (vv. 1-3)

"It pleased Darius to set over the [Medo-Persian] kingdom an hundred and twenty princes, who should be over the whole kingdom; and over these, three presidents [lit., "chiefs"], of whom Daniel was first; that the princes might give accounts unto them, and the king should have no damage. Then this Daniel was preferred above the presidents and princes because an excellent spirit was in him; and the king thought to set him over the whole realm."

A. The Superior Authority Over Daniel

Notice that Darius was the king who ruled Medo-Persia. Since no known extrabiblical data that speaks of Darius exists, we don't know for certain who he is. We find no one named Darius in any of the genealogical records of the kings of that time.

Some scholars believe that Darius is another name for a ruler by the name of Gubaru, who was appointed by Cyrus to govern the territory of Babylon while Cyrus himself ruled the whole Medo-Persian Empire. But the explanation that I prefer is that Darius is another name for Cyrus.

1. His title

The name *Darius* can serve as a title, like pharaoh, king, or Caesar. The word *Darius* has been found by archaeologists on inscriptions for at least five different Persian rulers. Since it seems best to see this as a title of honor or significance, we can assume it was a title given to Cyrus.

If you look at verse 28 of this chapter we might see Darius used in this way: "So this Daniel prospered in the reign of Darius, and ["even" in Aramaic] in the reign of Cyrus, the Persian."

2. His territory

Verse 1 says that Darius "set over the kingdom an hundred and twenty princes." If he were doing that, he would have to be bigger than a local ruler in Babylon. Furthermore, if he were going to establish three chiefs over the entire kingdom (v. 2), he'd have to be important. I believe Darius was the Medo-Persian monarch, Cyrus, identified by his official title.

3. His traits

Cyrus, or Darius, was a capable, intelligent, and powerful man who was an effective organizer and administrator. Though he was a man without a commitment to the true God, he did reveal a great interest in the God of Daniel.

B. The Special Abilities of Daniel

Verse 2 says, "Over these [120 princes was set], three presidents, of whom Daniel was first." Though it is possible to translate "first" as "one," it could also mean that he was the first one chosen or the first in rank. We don't know which is best, but the point is made that "Daniel was preferred above the presidents and princes, because an excellent spirit was in him" (v. 3). The word *preferred* in the Aramaic is a participle, which shows us that Daniel was constantly distinguishing himself over the others.

1. He was a fine statesman

Daniel was the finest statesman of the two empires in which he served.

2. He possessed the right attitude

His "excellent spirit" refers to his attitude, which was truly commendable.

3. He had previous experience

Having lived through the previous regime as prime minister, Daniel acquired:

a) Wisdom

b) A sense of history

c) Dramatic leadership ability evidenced by the model he set for his three friends (Dan. 1)

d) Administrative ability

e) The ability to interpret dreams and receive visions

C. The Strategic Appointment of Daniel

God allowed Darius to recognize Daniel's abilities and to put him in a strategic position. In the first year of his reign, Cyrus (Darius) issued a decree to the Jews to return to Judah after seventy years of Babylonian captivity (Ezra 1:1-3). I believe Cyrus made the decree because of Daniel's wisdom and influence. Although Daniel was old by this time (nearly ninety), he was still God's man chosen by the king to be prime minister. Even had the king desired to retain someone else as prime minister, he would not have been able to withstand God's sovereign plan.

II. THE PLOT (vv. 4-9)

Whenever a man is exalted by the Lord to a place of prominence, he falls into certain difficulty. There is always a price to pay. People inevitably are envious of such a position. We find that critical spirit recorded in Philippians 1: Paul was a prisoner and some were adding affliction to his bonds by saying evil things about his ministry (vv. 28-30). When God exalts people, the hearts of many others burn in rage, jealousy, and bitterness, even when that individual has done them no injury or harm. How could anyone despise such a man as Daniel, let alone crucify one such as Jesus Christ?

A. The Conspiracy (v. 4)

"Then the presidents and princes sought to find occasion against Daniel concerning the kingdom; but they could find no occasion nor fault, forasmuch as he was faithful, neither was there any error or fault found in him."

Being intensely jealous of Daniel, his enemies sought to bring charges against him. But Daniel had no skeletons in his closet. When one's peers are unable to find something wrong with someone who had served in office as long as Daniel had, then that individual must have great integrity, honesty, and purity. Daniel's enemies could find no "fault" (Aram., *shehitah*, "corruption") or "error" (Aram., *shalu*, "neglect") in him.

B. The Conclusion (v. 5)

"Then said these men, We shall not find any occasion against this Daniel, except we find it against him concerning the law of his God."

When people are unable to condemn you for anything but being sold out to God, then you are fulfilling the New Testament principle of suffering "for righteousness' sake" (Matt. 5:10-12). Daniel's enemies concluded, "The only thing we'll ever get on him is that he is totally committed to his God." What a commendation!

C. The Consultation (vv. 6-7)

"Then these presidents and princes assembled together to the king, and said thus unto him, King Darius, live forever. All the presidents of the kingdom, the governors, and the princes, the counselors, and the captains, have consulted together to establish a royal statute, and to make a firm decree, that whosoever shall ask a petition of any god or man for thirty days, except of thee, O king, shall be cast into the den of lions."

That the officials "assembled together" (v. 6) implies from the Aramaic that they came hastily and tumultuously. I'm sure he wasn't even consulted about this "royal statute, and . . . firm decree," which they wanted to be as binding as possible.

The Gods Who Were Created in Man's Image

Ancient religions typically established deities that were as fallible as men because they created God in their own image. It is absolutely ludicrous for us to say a man could become a god because we understand God to be holy and righteous. But that was a problem for these ancient pagans. In fact, history records that the Egyptians believed the pharaohs were gods; the Romans believed the Caesars were gods; and the kings of the Ptolemies and Seleucids were called gods as well. You may even remember the people exalting Herod as having "the voice of a god" (Acts 12:22). It was not uncommon for monarchs to be considered gods.

Darius was flattered. After all, when you have the whole political body wanting to exalt you as god, it's difficult to resist.

D. The Commitment (vv. 8-9)

"Now, O king, establish the decree, and sign the writing, that it be not charged, according to the law of the Medes and Persians, which altereth not. Wherefore, King Darius signed the writing and the decree."

Though we don't know much about the Medes and Persians, we do know that once a law was made, they could not alter it. Because the laws were binding, they were careful about the ones they legislated. But when the political leaders appealed to the king's ego, they were able to pass this law: if you made a petition of any god but Darius you would go to the lions' den.

III. THE PERSEVERANCE (vv. 10-11)

"Now when Daniel knew that the writing was signed, he went into his house; and his windows being opened in his chamber toward Jerusalem, he kneeled upon his knees three times a day, and prayed, and gave thanks before his God, as he did previously. Then these men assembled, and found Daniel praying and making supplication before his God."

A. The Pattern Established

A law was made prohibiting prayer to God, but Daniel went back to his room and did what he had always done. He continued to follow the pattern established by David as recorded in Psalm 55:17, "Evening, and morning, and at noon, will I pray." Houses in Babylon often had lattice-work over the windows to allow ventilation in the hot climate. It was through that latticework that Daniel would have been visible as he faced Jerusalem and prayed for its restoration.

B. The Priority Established

When men make laws that violate the higher laws that God has laid down, we don't have to follow them. That was Peter's response in Acts 5:29 when he said, "We ought to obey God rather than men."

Couldn't Daniel have been a little more discreet by closing the shutters before he prayed? Yes, but any compromise at all would have been seen as self-serving, and it wasn't in his character to do that.

The Perseverance of Polycarp Under the Persecution

When Polycarp, the bishop of Smyrna, was burned at the stake around A.D. 156, he had been a Christian for eighty-six years. Before the fire was lit, Polycarp's executioners called on him to deny the Lord and save his life. He answered, "Eighty and six years have I served him, and he never once wronged me; how then shall I blaspheme my King, who hath saved me?" (*Fox's Book of Martyrs*, ed. William Byron Forbush [Philadelphia: Universal Book and Bible House, 1926], p. 9). Polycarp, the disciple of the apostle John, with praises on his lips in quiet commitment to the Lord, looked down at the flames and accepted them as God's will.

IV. THE PROSECUTION (vv. 12-14)

A. The Accusation of Daniel

1. The violation clarified

"Then they came near, and spoke before the king concerning the king's decree" (v. 12*a*). The officials behind the plot probably had the decree signed in the morning, spied out Daniel at noon, and then ran back to the king to report what they saw. They asked him, "Hast thou not signed a decree, that every man that shall ask a petition of any god or man within thirty days, except of thee, O king, shall be cast into the den of lions? The king answered and said, The thing is true, according to the law of the Medes and Persians, which altereth not" (v. 12*b*).

2. The violator identified

"Then answered they and said before the king, That Daniel, who is of the children of the captivity of Judah [a foreigner and not even of the right stock], regardeth not thee, O king" (v. 13*a*). That wasn't true! Daniel was a loyal and faithful servant as long as he never had to violate his principles. He regarded the king in the proper manner, rendering "unto Caesar the things which are Caesar's" (Matt. 22:21). The officials continued their accusation: "[Daniel ignores] the decree that thou hast signed, but maketh his petition three times a day" (v. 13*b*). I'm sure they didn't see all three violations. After observing one they immediately assumed he would continue to pray three times a day.

B. The Attempt of Deliverance

Though it was a foolish thing to have done, the king admitted he was at fault: "Then the king, when he heard these words, was very much displeased with himself" (v. 14*a*). He was honest enough to put the blame where it belonged—on himself.

In response to his deep regret, the king "set his heart on Daniel to deliver him; and he labored till the going down of the sun to deliver him" (v. 14b). If the accusation of Daniel had been made after noon, then the king would have had the rest of the day to have Daniel acquitted, because execution, according to their custom, had to occur before nightfall. He exhausted every legal means trying to find a loophole in the law or some legal precedent that could reverse the decision. But he found none.

C. The Absence of Defense

Daniel never defended himself before his accusers. Like Christ, he was dumb before his shearers, not opening his mouth (Isa. 53:7; cf. Acts 8:32-35). Daniel had such confidence in God that he committed himself to Him and made no defense. Nothing remained to say but to admit he had been praying.

V. THE PENALTY (vv. 15-17)

A. The Implementation of Darius's Law (vv. 15-16a)

"Then these men assembled unto the king, and said unto the king, Know, O king, that the law of the Medes and Persians is, that no decree nor statute which the king establisheth may be changed. Then the king commanded, and they brought Daniel, and cast him into the den of lions."

1. The number of lions

Now, these lions were purposely starved to be used as executioners. We don't know how many lions were in the den. But there must have been many because when all the enemies of Daniel who designed the plot were thrown into the den with their families, they were overtaken before they reached the ground.

2. The den of lions

What exactly was this den of lions like? It most likely was a cave in the side of a hill that had been enlarged. At "the mouth of the den" (v. 17) a stone covered the opening. Above the cave another opening was covered with a grate. The reason many believe the den was underground is that the Aramaic word for den (*gob*) is related to the Hebrew word *gub*, meaning "to dig [a pit]." The cave's natural side entrance would have been used for bringing in the lions and maintaining the den. The top opening would have been for ventilation and watching executions.

B. The Impact of Daniel's Life (vv. 16*b*-17)

"Now the king spoke and said unto Daniel, Thy God, whom thou servest continually, he will deliver thee" (v. 16*b*).

Where would the king have concluded that idea? If Daniel had already been serving in the king's court for a year or two, then Darius must have heard message after message about God from Daniel. The king might have also heard the history of what Daniel's God had done in the past. It's apparent that Daniel would have expressed what he believed. For example, I'm sure he talked about how God delivered Shadrach, Meshach, and Abednego from the fiery furnace. The king's response shows that Daniel's evangelistic efforts had some impact.

In spite of the king's positive attitude toward Daniel, however, the penalty still had to be carried out: "A stone was brought, and laid upon the mouth of the den; and the king sealed it with his own signet, and with the signet of his lords, that the purpose might not be changed concerning Daniel" (v. 17). Neither party could break that double seal.

VI. THE PRESERVATION (vv. 18-23)

A. The Anxiety of Darius (vv. 18-20)

"Then the king went to his palace" (v. 18). Throwing Daniel in the lions' den is the climax of the story. What are we doing in the king's palace? We get an insight into the king's deep concern for Daniel's welfare as he "passed the night fasting; neither were instruments of music [lit., "diversions," i.e., music, women, dancing]

113

brought before him; and his sleep went from him. Then the king arose very early in the morning [lit., "at the brightness of the dawning"], and went in haste unto the den of lions" (vv. 18b-19). The fact that Darius hurried to the den of lions at the crack of dawn to see what had happened indicates that he had some faith in the God of Daniel. "When he came to the den, he cried with a lamentable voice unto Daniel. And [hoping for the best but perhaps believing the worst,] the king spoke and said to Daniel, O Daniel, servant of the living God, is thy God, whom thou servest continually, able to deliver thee from the lions?" (v. 20).

B. The Answer of Daniel (vv. 21-23)

1. The verification (vv. 21-22a)

"Then said Daniel unto the king, O king, live forever. My God hath sent his angel, and hath shut the lions' mouths."

The angel apparently took care of the lions' paws too, otherwise they would have ripped him to shreds. Angels are so powerful that one slew 185,000 Assyrians by himself (2 Kings 19:35). One angel would certainly be enough to preserve Daniel's life.

2. The vindication (vv. 22b-23)

a) Reported (v. 22b)

"[The lions] have not hurt me, forasmuch as before him innocence was found in me; and also before thee, O king, have I done no hurt."

Those statements were not expressions of pride because they were true. Daniel defended himself only after God had put him through the test. He put his life in God's hands in that lions' den and waited for God to evaluate his innocence.

b) Realized (v. 23)

> "Then was the king exceedingly glad for him, and commanded that they should take Daniel up out of the den. So Daniel was taken up out of the den, and no manner of hurt was found upon him, because he believed in his God."

> Some ropes were probably dropped into the pit to pull up this nearly ninety-year-old man. Such a deliverance was a vindication of Daniel's great faith in God—he believed God, and God honored his faith.

But it doesn't always happen that way. Isaiah believed God, too, but he was sawn in half. Paul believed God, yet was beheaded. Peter believed God but was crucified upside down. Believing God doesn't mean that the lions will not devour you—martyrs throughout the history of God's dealing with men have believed God. We must accept God's will: if it is to live, we live; if it is to die, we die. But in either case we're never defeated. In fact, if Daniel had been eaten by the lions, he would have been in the presence of God.

VII. THE PUNISHMENT (v. 24)

> "The king commanded, and they brought those men who had accused Daniel, and they cast them into the den of lions, them, their children, and their wives; and the lions had the mastery of them, and broke all their bones in pieces before they came to the bottom of the den."

Strangely enough, some people say that Daniel didn't get eaten because the lions weren't hungry. But take note that they were hungry enough to eat this large group of people. Others have suggested that Daniel didn't get eaten because the lions were old. However, to say that is to read into the text. What this horrifying scene pictures is the retribution and vengeance of God. The Medes and Persians had a law stating that the guilt of one was to be shared by his kindred, so the families of the perpetrators of the plot perished as well.

VIII. THE PROCLAMATION (vv. 25-27)

A. The Servant of God (vv. 25-26a)

"Then King Darius wrote unto all people, nations, and languages that dwell in all the earth: Peace be multiplied unto you. I make a decree, that in every dominion of my kingdom men tremble and fear before the God of Daniel."

One man affected the entire empire: the whole Medo-Persian Empire was commanded to tremble in fear before the God of Daniel! It doesn't take a lot of people to make an impact—it merely takes the right kind.

B. The Sovereignty of God (v. 26b)

"For he is the living God, and steadfast forever, and his kingdom that which shall not be destroyed, and his dominion shall be even unto the end."

Darius may have been a pagan king, but he sounded like a psalmist. Nations may come and go, whether they be Babylonian or Medo-Persian. But when God puts His men in the right place, His message gets through.

C. The Salvation of God (v. 27)

"He delivereth and rescueth, and he worketh signs and wonders in heaven and in earth, who hath delivered Daniel from the power of the lions."

Who receives the glory in this chapter? Not Daniel—he just happened to be there. God received the glory. If one theme is extant throughout the book of Daniel, it is the majesty of God. He stands against the backdrop of the nations of the world and upholds His sovereignty.

IX. THE PROSPERITY (v. 28)

"So this Daniel prospered in the reign of Darius, and [or "even"] in the reign of Cyrus, the Persian."

Conclusion

As we look at this chapter and the first chapter in the book of Daniel, what do we learn about Daniel? In chapter 1 we saw him as a virtuous, godly young man. In chapter 6, which occurred about seventy years later, we still see the same uncompromising character. What are the elements of his character that we could apply to our own lives? What made Daniel so effective? Let me suggest some qualities.

1. He transcended history and consequently was an individual useful to God. Daniel pulled his feet out of the muck of human issues. He sought the kingdom of God.

2. He lived a consistent life from start to finish. Daniel was a virtuous man when he was young as well as when he was old. There is no simple way to humanly measure the power of such a virtuous life. The tragedy is that most of us find our virtue coming and going through the years.

3. He fulfilled his calling. He lived in the absolute center of God's will. His only desire was that God's will be done.

4. He had the right attitude. It was said of Daniel that he had "an excellent spirit" (Dan. 6:3).

5. He was envied and hated by the world around him, but was never embittered by it.

6. He was condemned for his righteousness. He was as an elder of a church should be—blameless (1 Tim. 3:2).

7. He was known for his virtue and integrity even by his enemies.

8. He was a faithful citizen. He abided by the law of the land and went against it only when it clearly violated the laws of God.

9. He was willing to face any consequence within the framework of God's will and leave the outcome to God.

10. He served faithfully no matter what it cost him personally.

11. He never defended himself; he left that to God.

12. He strengthened the faith of others by giving them hope in God. Even the king believed because of the great faith of Daniel.

13. He was delivered from all harm and was preserved for every purpose within the will of God.

14. He was a vehicle for God's glory. That is precisely what we, as Christians, are to be.

15. He was avenged by God. He didn't need to deal with his enemies himself.

16. He was exalted by those around him as well as by the One above him.

What great principles that show the virtuous life of a man of God!

Focusing on the Facts

1. How much does the rise and fall of nations affect the ongoing existence of the people of God? What illustrates that in Daniel's life (see p. 103)?
2. Compared to the sovereignty of God, how did Isaiah represent the nations in Isaiah 40:7-8, 15 (see pp. 103-4)?
3. What seems to be a good solution to the identity of Darius, and why (see pp. 105-6)?
4. What were some of the qualities by which Daniel distinguished himself (see pp. 106-7)?
5. What decree of Cyrus (Ezra 1:1-3) did Daniel possibly influence (see p. 107)?
6. What were the conspirators attempting to find in Daniel's life? Were they able to do so (see pp. 107-8)?
7. What was the only thing they were able to find "wrong" with Daniel (see p. 108)?
8. What made Darius vulnerable to accept the decree (see p. 109)?
9. According to the reasoning of Acts 5:29, why did Daniel continue to pray (see p. 110)?

10. Why did Daniel decide not to compromise his prayer life for thirty days (see p. 110)?
11. Daniel was a loyal and faithful servant as long as he never had to _____ his principles (see p. 111).
12. How did the king attempt to compensate for his foolish decision (see p. 112)?
13. Why did Daniel not take up his own defense (see p. 112)?
14. How did Darius get the idea that God would deliver Daniel (see p. 113)?
15. Why were Daniel's statements about the proof of his innocence not an expression of pride (see p. 114)?
16. What evidence do we have that believing in God does not guarantee we won't be killed under persecution? What is the primary issue (see p. 115)?
17. Why can't we ignore the miraculous nature of Daniel's deliverance (see p. 115)?
18. What does it take to make an impact (see p. 66)?
19. What is one theme that runs throughout the book of Daniel (see p. 116)?

Pondering the Principles

1. Have you evaluated your attitudes lately? Do you find yourself complaining about the way things are and how they should have been? Do you dwell on the obstacle rather than its solution? Would you like to cultivate that "excellent spirit" for which Daniel was noted (Dan. 6:3)? Read the following verses: Proverbs 12:25; 15:15; Romans 12:9-12; Philippians 2:1-4, 13-15. Do you think your attitudes depend on circumstances, or do you decide to have "an excellent spirit" no matter what happens? It might seem that with the persecution and imprisonment Paul was experiencing (see Phil. 1), he had the right to have a negative attitude. However, what truth did he record in Philippians 2:13 that allows us to accept circumstances without allowing them to destroy our positive outlook? What is the purpose of maintaining such an attitude (vv. 14-15)? Make a commitment to speak some encouraging words to those you will be seeing today, regardless of what pressures or problems you may be facing. Remember, if you are a Christian, "it is God who is at work in you . . . for His good pleasure" (Phil. 2:13, NASB).

2. Like Darius, have you made hasty decisions that you later regretted? Read Hebrews 12:16-17 (cf. Gen. 25:27-34) and Proverbs 21:5. Actions that are not well thought out can have damaging consequences. When you are faced with a major decision, do you "commit your way to the Lord" (Ps. 37:5, NASB) in prayer, seeking the counsel of wise and godly people (Prov. 24:6)? Carefully evaluate the impact that the decisions you are faced with will have on your testimony before the watching world and the glory of God.

3. Sometimes a fine line exists between presuming upon God's protection and refusing to compromise. If you had been faced with the decree that Daniel was, would you have altered your praying pattern for thirty days to prevent "rocking the boat"? Why or why not? Jesus was always careful not to presume upon God's promises (e.g., Matt. 4:6-7; Mark 3:7-9; John 6:15; 7:1); yet, when it came to God's reputation and glory, He was willing to confront the issue (e.g., John 2:14-17; Luke 22:42). Seek to do the same yourself, considering what Christ would do if He were in your situation.

4. Slowly look over the principles for living an uncompromising life (see pp. 117-18). Which are characteristic of your life? Which are you weak in? Pray that you would be challenged to see those areas strengthened. Write down your commitment so that you are consistently reminded of your goal.

Scripture Index

Topical Index

Abednego. *See* Shadrach, Meshach, and Abednego

Abrasiveness, avoiding, 27, 31, 56

Aesop, on compromise, 53

Alexander the Great, wine and, 43

America, dispensability of, 103

Amusement parks, idolatry and, 73

Babylon
food of, 26
language of, 21
religion of, 22-25, 26
sciences of, 22

Barnabas, uncompromising nature of, 15

Blamelessness. *See* Integrity

Boldness, 35-37, 44

Brainwashing, 22-25, 34-35

"Cadet Prayer," 53

Chaldea. *See* Babylon

Commitment, 14-15, 23-27, 35, 44, 50, 52-54, 58, 61, 84-98, 107-18, 120

Compromise
Christians and, 10-14, 29-30, 50-51, 100
consequences of, 12-13, 44-46, 53-55
definition of, 11, 26
examples of, 51-52
lack of respect for, 44, 84
process of, 84
protection of God and, 44-46
rationalization of, 84
reasons for, 50-51, 84
refusal to. *See* Commitment

societal, 9-10, 29-30, 87

Convictions. *See* Commitment

Courage. *See* Boldness

Criswell, W. A., wine and history, 43

Cyrus. *See* Darius

Daniel
age of, 19-20, 25
appearance of, 20
attributes of. *See* characteristics of
blessing on, 59-60, 116
boldness of, 35-37
characteristics of, 106-7, 117-18
dating book of, 77
deportation of, 16-19
education of, 19-26, 59
faith of, 57-58, 112
influence of, 44, 61, 103-5, 113, 116
integrity of, 108, 117
intellect of, 20, 59
Joseph and, 55
marital status of, 18
noble status of, 18-19
nonabrasive nature of, 27-28, 56
persistence of, 55-57
prayer and, 108-10
protection of, 43-46, 113-15
social skills of, 20-21
standard of, 39-40
survival of, 103-5
superiority of, 60-61, 106
testing of, 58-59, 112-15
uncompromising nature of, 15, 23-27, 35, 44, 52, 57-58, 61, 107-18

125

witness of. *See* influence of

Darius
　haste of, 109-12, 120
　honesty of, 111-12
　identity of, 105-6
　pride of, 109

David
　boldness of, 37
　uncompromising nature of,
　　15

Deliverance, miraculous, 90-92,
　115

Drinking
　abstaining from, 40-43
　danger of, 43
　history affected by, 43
　neutrality of, 40

Education
　benefit of secular, 25, 34-35
　brainwashing and, 23-25, 34

Eli, compromise of, 54-55

Envy. *See* Jealousy

Eunuchs, 18

Evangelism
　avoiding abrasive, 27-28, 31
　personal influence and, 44,
　　61, 103-5, 113, 116

Expediency. *See* Compromise

Food, enslavement to, 23-24

Gluttony. *See* Food

God
　protection of. *See* Protection
　sovereignty of, 103, 116
　will of. *See* Will of God

Government
　mortality of nations, 102-4
　obedience to, 88-90, 94

Haste, folly of, 108-11, 120

History, direction of, 102-5, 116

Holiness, 14-15. *See also* Integrity, Separation

Honor. *See* Integrity

"How Firm a Foundation," 98

Hurry. *See* Haste

Idolatry
　church, 74
　condemnation of, 68-70
　consequences of, 70-71
　definition of, 71
　explanation of, 66-68
　gods in man's image, 109
　illustrations of, 66-67
　Israel's, 74-75
　manifestations of, 69-70
　modern, 71-74, 81
　punishments for, 71
　responding against, 76-80
　seriousness of, 71

Integrity, 27, 80-81, 108, 117. *See also* Commitment

Intimidation. *See* Compromise

Jealousy
　backfiring of, 97-98, 115
　danger of, 88, 107-8
　sin of, 88

Jesus Christ, uncompromising nature of, 14

Job, uncompromising nature of, 91-93

Joseph, Daniel and, 55

Kreisler, Fritz, 27-28

Liddell, Eric, 53-54, 62

Luther, Martin, uncompromising nature of, 92

McDowell, Josh, dating book of Daniel, 77

Meshach. *See* Shadrach, Meshach, and Abednego

Moody Press, a ministry of the Moody Bible Institute, is designed for education, evangelization, and edification. If we may assist you in knowing more about Christ and the Christian life, please write us without obligation: Moody Press, c/o MLM, Chicago, Illinois 60610.